THE UK Weber's BBQ COOKBOOK 2023

Simple, Delicious Recipes and Techniques for the World's Best Barbecue

Riley Singh

Copyright ©2022 By Riley Singh All rights reserved.

No part of this guide may be reproduced in any form without permission in writing from the publisher except in the case of brief quotations embodied in critical articles or reviews.

Legal & Disclaimer

The information contained in this book and its contents is not designed to replace or take the place of any form of medical or professional advice; and is not meant to replace the need for independent medical, financial, legal or other professional advice or services, as may be required. The content and information in this book has been provided for educational and entertainment purposes only.

The content and information contained in this book has been compiled from sources deemed reliable, and it is accurate to the best of the Author's knowledge, information and belief. However, the Author cannot guarantee its accuracy and validity and cannot be held liable for any errors and/or omissions. Further, changes are periodically made to this book as and when needed. Where appropriate and/or necessary, you must consult a professional (including but not limited to your doctor, attorney, financial advisor or such other professional advisor) before using any of the suggested remedies, techniques, or information in this book.

Contents

INTRODUCTION 5

BEEF RECIPES 8

Braised Short Ribs 9
Sloppy Joes 10
Wild Mushroom And Blue Cheese Stuffed Burger 11
Asian Beef & Mushroom Tacos 12
Newfoundland Moose Stew 13
Banh Mi Burger 14
Seared Beef Spinalis 15
Italian Spaghetti Sauce And Meatballs 16
Smoked Beef Tenderloin 17
Mini Lamb Sliders With Tzatziki Sauce 18
Bacon Cheeseburger Hotdogs 19

POULTRY RECIPES 20

Grilled Duck Breast With Apple Brandy Glaze ...21
Green Curry Chicken 23
Blueberry Bbq Chicken 24
Company Cornish Game Hens 25
Duck And Mango Quesadilla 26
Paella 27
Tandoori Chicken 28
Braised Chicken Thighs With Mushrooms 29
Chicken Keema Burgers 30
Country Chicken Saltimbocca 31
Spatchcocked Chicken Two Ways 32

PORK RECIPES 33

Blt Soup 34
Prosciutto Wrapped Cheese Dogs 35
Duck & Potatoes 36
Pork Tortas Ahogada 38
Takeo Spikes' Ribs 39
Christmas Gingersnap Ham 40
The Perfect Gift For Your Favorite Egghead 41
Barbecued Pork Shoulder With Carolina Sauce 42
Pulled Pork Sandwiches 43
Bacon-wrapped Pig Wings 44
Leg Of Warthog 45

FISH AND SEAFOOD RECIPES 46

Grilled Oysters 47
Grilled Asian Mahi-mahi 48
Smoked King Salmon 49
Grilled Fish Tacos With Peach Salsa 50
Arctic Char With Blood Orange Salad 51
Maple-glazed Applewood Smoked Octopus 52
Raspberry Glazed Salmon 53
Swordfish Steaks With Peach Salsa 54

Seared Tuna 55	Bourbon-glazed Cold Smoked Salmon 57
Miso Poached Sea Bass 56	

BURGERS RECIPES 58

Breakfast Burger...59	Quesadilla Burger..62
Classic American Burger 60	The Crowned Jewels Burger 63
Oahu Burger 61	"the Masterpiece"...64

DESSERTS RECIPES 65

Seasonal Fruit Cobbler.....................................66	Berry Upside-down Cake..................................70
Fresh Peach Crisp..67	Death By Chocolate...71
S'mores Pizza..67	Grilled Pineapple Sundaes 72
Grilled Sopapillas...68	Chocolate Chip Cookie Peanut Butter C.
Apple Pizza...68	S'mores 72
Corn & Jalapeño Focaccia 69	

SIDES RECIPES 73

Ratatouille..74	Cowboy Potatoes 80
Roasted Potatoes 75	Mac And Cheese 81
Grilled Lemon Garlic Zucchini 76	Grilled Cabbage With Champagne Vinaigrette..82
Smoked Potato Salad......................................77	Dutch Oven Black Beans..................................83
Grilled Onions...78	
Baba Ganoush...79	

INTRODUCTION

CHARCOAL GRILLING 101: A GUIDE TO GETTING THAT PERFECT SEAR EVERY TIME

There's nothing like smell of a charcoal grill being fired up to get us salivating and ready to celebrate summer — but charcoal grilling can be intimidating. How do you start it? Where's the best spot for the food? When do you open the vents? Well, no need to worry — we've got you covered on the basics of grilling with charcoal.

HOW TO START A CHARCOAL GRILL

Traditional briquettes are inexpensive, light easily and burn long and steady. If you want a more intense, smoky flavor, go with hardwood charcoal (aka lump charcoal). These are blazingly hot but burn out faster.

Before you even light your grill, make sure to open to vents. The fire will need oxygen to keep going. After the charcoals are placed in the barbecue, you can control the internal cooking temperature by adjusting the vents: wider vents means hotter flames and more oxygen, while smaller vents means a cooler cooking temperature. Never close them all the way or the flames will go out.

Start your grill with a charcoal chimney; this is the easiest way to get your charcoal going. You do not need lighter fluid.

Stuff newspaper loosely in the bottom of the chimney (there is a space for it under the wire rack), then fill the chimney with charcoal. Remove top grate from grill, place chimney inside, and light the newspaper.

But how long should you let the coals burn? Let the charcoal or briquettes burn until they're covered with white-gray ash (it takes about 5 to 10 minutes for the coals to get to high heat and 25 to 30 minutes to get to medium heat).

Take the top grate of your grill off and, wearing protective grill gloves, hold the chimney by its handles and pour charcoal into the grill. Then take a paper towel soaked in vegetable oil, and spread it over grate with tongs. This is the trick to keep food from sticking to the grill.

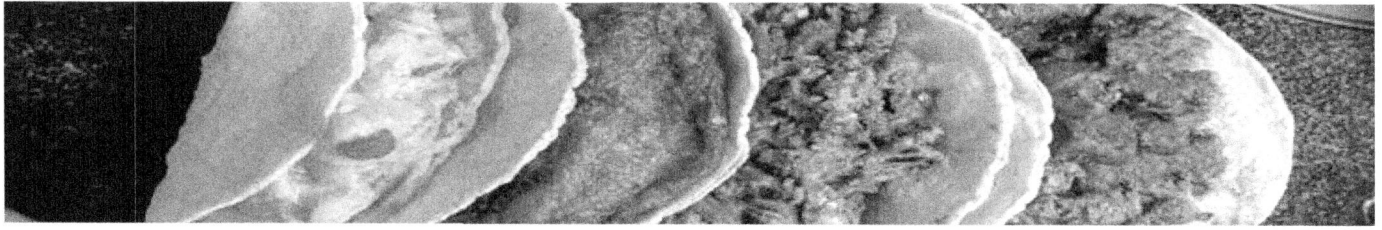

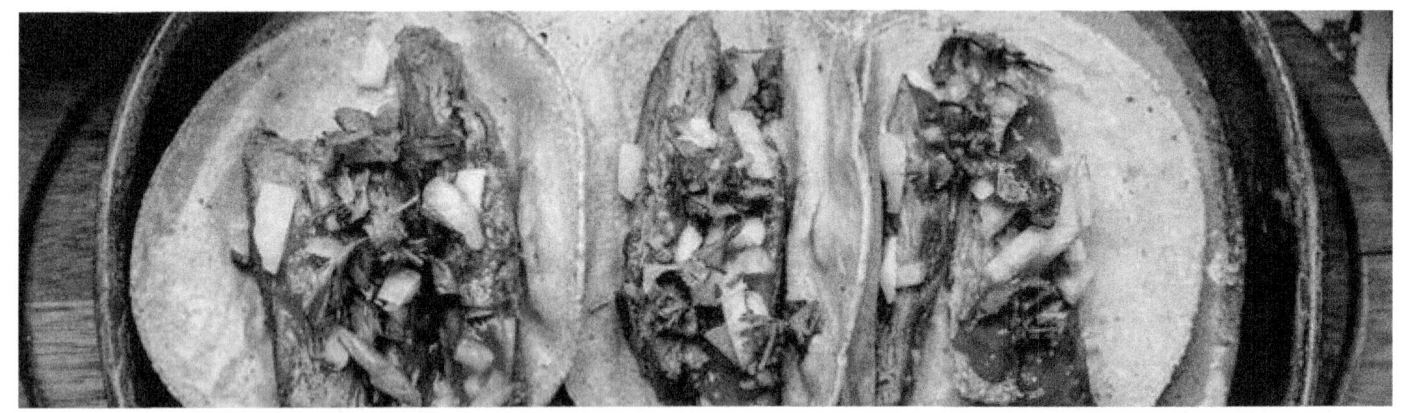

CHARCOAL GRILLING 101: A GUIDE TO GETTING THAT PERFECT SEAR EVERY TIME

There's nothing like smell of a charcoal grill being fired up to get us salivating and ready to celebrate summer — but charcoal grilling can be intimidating. How do you start it? Where's the best spot for the food? When do you open the vents? Well, no need to worry — we've got you covered on the basics of grilling with charcoal.

HOW TO START A CHARCOAL GRILL

Traditional briquettes are inexpensive, light easily and burn long and steady. If you want a more intense, smoky flavor, go with hardwood charcoal (aka lump charcoal). These are blazingly hot but burn out faster.

Before you even light your grill, make sure to open to vents. The fire will need oxygen to keep going. After the charcoals are placed in the barbecue, you can control the internal cooking temperature by adjusting the vents: wider vents means hotter flames and more oxygen, while smaller vents means a cooler cooking temperature. Never close them all the way or the flames will go out.

Start your grill with a charcoal chimney; this is the easiest way to get your charcoal going. You do not need lighter fluid.

Stuff newspaper loosely in the bottom of the chimney (there is a space for it under the wire rack), then fill the chimney with charcoal. Remove top grate from grill, place chimney inside, and light the newspaper.

But how long should you let the coals burn? Let the charcoal or briquettes burn until they're covered with white-gray ash (it takes about 5 to 10 minutes for the coals to get to high heat and 25 to 30 minutes to get to medium heat).

Take the top grate of your grill off and, wearing protective grill gloves, hold the chimney by its handles and pour charcoal into the grill. Then take a paper towel soaked in vegetable oil, and spread it over grate with tongs. This is the trick to keep food from sticking to the grill.

WHAT TO GRILL ON LOW HEAT

Christopher Arturo, Culinary Arts chef-instructor at the Institute of Culinary Education, does not recommend grilling at low heat (about 300 degrees) on a charcoal grill for the whole time because the protein will likely dry out. That being said, there are certain foods that do well cooked on high heat and then transferred to an area of the grill at low heat. Folks can do this with larger pieces of protein, like pork chops, as well as fattier fishes like salmon. Arturo also loves grilling a whole onion with this method.

HOW TO CLEAN A CHARCOAL GRILL

Clean the grill right after cooking, while it's still hot, using a stiff-wire grill brush. Use it every time you grill to remove food particles from the cooking surface.

If you're looking for an alternative to using wire brushes (that may leave small wires and bits of metal behind), rub your grill grates with a peeled half onion," pitmaster Megan Day told TODAY Food. "Allow the grill to heat up to a high temperature. Pierce the half onion with a fork and rub the cut-side down along the grill grates. The onion's juices will release and produce steam to remove the bits and charred on debris."

BEEF RECIPES

Braised Short Ribs

 Servings: 8   Cooking Time: 130 Mins.

Ingredients:

- 8 bone-in beef short ribs
- 1 tsp salt
- 2 tsp freshly ground black pepper
- 4 tbsp olive oil
- ½ C. yellow onion, diced
- 3 cloves garlic, minced
- 1 C. beef broth
- 3 tbsp Worcestershire sauce
- 1 C. red wine
- 2 sprigs of rosemary

Directions:

1. Preheat the grill to 350°F using direct heat with a cast iron grate installed.
2. Season the short ribs with salt and pepper. Heat olive oil in the dutch oven. Sear short ribs for 1 minute per side. Remove from the dutch oven and set aside.
3. Add the onion to the dutch oven and cook for 3 minutes or until it is translucent. Add in garlic and cook for an additional minute.
4. Pour beef broth, Worcestershire sauce and red wine into the dutch oven. Bring to a simmer and add in the short ribs. Place the rosemary sprigs on top. Cover the dutch oven and cook for 2½ hours, or until meat is tender.

Sloppy Joes

 Servings: 4   **Cooking Time: 40 Mins.**

Ingredients:

- 1 lb. ground beef
- 1/4 C. onion, finely chopped
- 1/4 C. bell pepper, finely chopped
- 1 clove garlic, finely chopped
- 1/2 C. tomato sauce
- 1/4 C. ketchup
- 2 tbsp. brown sugar
- 1 tbsp. brown mustard
- Salt & Pepper

Directions:

1. Preheat the grill to 400°F using direct heat with a cast iron grate installed with the dutch oven on the grid.
2. Place all ingredients in the dutch oven and stir.
3. Cover the dutch oven and lower the dome for 30-40 minutes or until the beef is cooked through.
4. Serve on hamburger buns.

Wild Mushroom And Blue Cheese Stuffed Burger

 Servings: 4   Cooking Time: 10 Mins.

Ingredients:

- 2 lbs (900 g) ground venison or sirloin
- Salt and pepper, for seasoning
- 2 1/2 tbsp (37 ml) hot sauce
- 10 oz (285 g) mixed wild mushrooms, sautéed and drained
- 8 oz (115 g) blue cheese, crumbled
- Arugula for garnish

Directions:

1. Mix the hot sauce into the ground meat, then divide the meat into eight equal portions, 1/4 lb. (113 g) each. Take one of the divided ground meat and form it in a small cup.
2. Fill center with the mushrooms and 6 oz (90 g) blue cheese. Place remaining ground meat on top and seal.
3. Preheat the grill to 400°F using direct heat with a cast iron grate installed. Cook burgers for 3 to 5 minutes per side depending on desired doneness. Top with remaining blue cheese and arugula.

Asian Beef & Mushroom Tacos

 Servings: 4   Cooking Time: 25 Mins.

Ingredients:

- ½ head of green cabbage
- 1 lb. (450g) flank or round steak, cut into very thin strips
- kosher salt and freshly ground black pepper
- 3 tbsp vegetable oil, divided
- 1 lb. (450g) white mushrooms, sliced
- 4 oz (110g) shredded carrots, fresh or pickled
- ⅓ C. hoisin sauce, plus more for serving
- 8 x 6-in (15.25-cm) flour tortillas
- ¼ C. chopped fresh cilantro

Directions:

1. Preheat the grill to 425°F (218°C) using direct heat with a standard grate installed and a cast iron skillet on the grate. Place cabbage on the grate (not in the skillet) cut side down, close the lid, and grill until beginning to soften and char, about 7 to 10 minutes. Remove cabbage from the grill and slice finely. Set aside.
2. Season beef well with salt and pepper. Add 2 tbsp oil to the hot skillet and heat until shimmering. Add beef and cook until the meat has browned on both sides, about 5 to 6 minutes, turning once. Transfer to a platter and set aside. Return the skillet to the grill.
3. Add the remaining 1 tbsp oil to the skillet and heat until shimmering. Add mushrooms and cook until they're tender and all the liquid has evaporated, about 5 minutes. Add carrots and sliced cabbage to the skillet and cook until beginning to soften, about 2 minutes, stirring once or twice. Add the hoisin sauce and beef, stir to coat, and cook for 1 minute more.
4. Remove the taco mixture from the grill. To serve, scoop an equal portion of the mixture into each tortilla and top with cilantro and more hoisin sauce (if desired).

Newfoundland Moose Stew

 Servings: 8   Cooking Time: 108 Mins.

Ingredients:

- One 2 lb. (900 g) moose or sirloin tip roast
- 6 sprigs thyme
- 2 bay leaves
- Zest of 1 lemon and 1 orange
- 12 oz (340 g) applewood-smoked bacon, cut into small strips (about 14 slices)
- 2 C. (480 ml) each of diced carrots, celery and onions
- Kosher salt and freshly ground black pepper
- 1 tbsp (15 ml) minced garlic
- 2 tbsp (30 ml) all-purpose flour
- Four 12 oz (360 ml) bottles lager
- 1 tsp (5 ml) ground coriander
- 9 C. (2.1 L) water
- 3 C. (710 ml) diced russet potatoes
- 2 C. (480 ml) diced Roma tomatoes
- 2 tbsp (30 ml) freshly squeezed lemon juice
- ¼ C. (60 ml) freshly squeezed orange juice
- ¼ C. (60 ml) unsalted butter
- ½ C. (120 ml) frozen peas
- ½ C. (120 ml) thinly sliced fresh chives

Directions:

1. Preheat the grill to 500°F using direct heat with a cast iron grate installed. Place the dutch oven on the grid to preheat for 10 minutes.
2. Trim the meat, cut into bite-sized cubes and set aside. To make a seasoning sachet, put the thyme, bay leaves, lemon zest and orange zest on a small piece of cheesecloth, pull up the sides and tie with string. Set aside. Add the bacon to the dutch oven and cook for 6 minutes or until crisp. Transfer the bacon to a plate lined with paper towels and set aside. Reserve the bacon fat in the dutch oven. Add the carrots, celery and onions to the dutch oven and cook until caramelized and golden brown in color. Remove the vegetables with a slotted spoon and place them in a small bowl.
3. Allow the dutch oven to reheat for about 2 minutes. Season the meat with salt and pepper and add to the dutch oven. Sear on all sides for about 10 minutes, or until brown. Add the garlic and cook for one minute, then add the flour and stir. Slowly add the lager, one bottle at a time. Add the reserved sachet and bacon and the coriander and stir well. Cover the dutch oven and simmer for 30 minutes.
4. Reduce the heat to 300°F. After 30 minutes, add 3 C. of water, cover the dutch oven and simmer for 30 minutes. Add 3 more C. of water, cover and simmer for 15 more minutes. Add 1 more C. of water, cover and simmer for another 15 minutes. Add the potatoes, tomatoes and reserved carrots, celery and onions. Add the remaining 2 C. of water, cover and simmer for another 30 minutes. Remove the dutch oven from the heat; discard the sachet and add the lemon juice, orange juice, butter, peas and chives. Season with salt and pepper. Serve immediately.

Banh Mi Burger

 Servings: 4   Cooking Time: 6 Mins.

Ingredients:

- 2 carrots, julienned or spiralized
- 1 small bunch radishes, thinly sliced
- 1 jalapeño, thinly sliced (optional)
- ¼ C. rice wine vinegar
- 2 tbsp. sugar
- ¼ C. mayonnaise
- 1 clove garlic
- 2 tbsp. Sriracha or sambal
- 1 tbsp. fresh lime juice
- salt and pepper
- 1 ½ lb. ground beef (preferably 80% lean)
- 1 tbsp. canola oil
- 4 slices cheddar cheese
- 4 Cobblestone Bread Co.™ Kaiser Rolls
- Mint, Thai basil, and cilantro

Directions:

1. Combine the carrots, radishes, and jalapeño in a mixing bowl and toss with the vinegar and sugar. Set aside. In a medium bowl, combine the mayonnaise, garlic, Sriracha, and lime juice. Season with salt and pepper and set that aside as well.
2. Divide the beef into 4 equal portions about 6 ounces each. Form each portion into a ¾ inch thick burger, making a depression in the center with your hand. Season with salt and pepper, and brush the burgers lightly with oil.
3. Preheat the grill to 450°F using direct heat with a cast iron grate installed. Grill the burgers for 3 minutes on the first side, until slightly charred and golden. Flip the burgers and cook on the other side for another 3 minutes. Top with the cheese and cook for another minute (for medium rare. You can adjust the cooking times according to your desired doneness).
4. Meanwhile, place the rolls on the kamado grill cut-side down and lightly toast for a couple minutes.
5. By now, your burgers should be done. Remove from the kamado grill and tent with foil to allow them to rest for a minute. Spread the spicy mayo onto each roll, and top with the burgers. Then top with your pickled vegetable mix and herbs. Serve!

Seared Beef Spinalis

 Servings: 4   Cooking Time: 55 Mins.

Ingredients:

- Spinalis steak
- 3 sprigs rosemary
- Steak seasoning
- 10 Hakerai turnips with tops, cut ¼ inch thick and roughly chopped greens
- 2 C. heavy cream
- 1 bay leaf
- 4 sprigs thyme
- 1 yellow onion, julienned
- 3 C. crushed Ritz crackers
- 1 C. pecorino cheese
- 2 C. dried morel mushrooms
- 3 bell peppers, any color
- Half a yellow onion, diced
- ½ C. basil, minced
- ½ C. sherry vinegar
- ½ C. olive oil
- Fresh ground black pepper
- Salt

Directions:

1. Preheat the grill to 275°F using direct heat with a cast iron grate installed.
2. Season all sides of the spinalis with your favorite steak seasoning – clean any of the hard-fatty tissue on the inside. Roll the steak and tie it together with butcher's twine. Take the rosemary sprigs and tuck underneath the string for cooking.
3. Cook the steak until it reaches an internal temperature of 120°F. Remove the steak from the grill and let it rest 15 minutes.
4. Set the kamado grill for direct cooking without a platesetter at 600°F.
5. Heat a cast iron pan in the kamado grill for 10 minutes. Sear the steak on all sides; remove and rest another 10 minutes. Slice and serve.
6. Set the kamado grill for indirect cooking with a platesetter at 300°F.
7. Add the heavy cream to a pot with bay leaf, thyme and salt and pepper. Bring the cream to a boil and let the herbs steep.
8. Add the turnips, their greens and onions to a bowl with the hot cream. Discard the thyme and bay leaf. Mix the contents of the bowl and add them to a cast iron skillet. Arrange the turnips in a shingled pattern.
9. In a separate bowl mix the chopped morels and pecorino cheese and the crackers. Top the gratin with the crackers mixture and spread evenly. Cook in the grill for 45 minutes; check the doneness with a toothpick. If the toothpick can be inserted without any resistance the gratin is done.
10. Set the kamado grill for direct cooking without a platesetter at 500°F.
11. Grill the whole peppers until the it is charred on each side and the skin is blistered. After the peppers have cooled, deseed the peppers, leaving the charred skin on and dice.
12. Add the bell pepper to a bowl with the rest of the ingredients and mix together. This is a wonderful steak topping.

Italian Spaghetti Sauce And Meatballs

 Servings: 12   Cooking Time: 120 Mins.

Ingredients:

- 1 lb. lean ground beef
- 1 C. Italian-style breadcrumbs
- 3 tbsp grated Parmesan cheese
- 3 tbsp. fresh parsley, chopped
- 1 clove garlic, minced
- ¼ tsp freshly ground black pepper
- 1 egg, beaten
- 1 medium onion, chopped
- 4 cloves garlic, divided, minced
- 1/4 C. olive oil
- 2 (28 ounce) cans whole peeled tomatoes
- 1 tsp white sugar
- 1½ tsp salt
- 1 bay leaf
- 1 (6 ounce) can tomato paste
- ¾ tsp dried basil
- ½ tsp freshly ground black pepper

Directions:

1. In a large bowl, combine the ground beef, breadcrumbs, cheese, parsley, garlic, black pepper and beaten egg. Mix well and form into 12 balls. Cover and store in the refrigerator until needed.
2. Preheat the grill to 350°F using direct heat with a cast iron grate installed. Add a cast iron skillet to preheat, then sauté the garlic and onion in olive oil until the onion is translucent. Stir in the tomatoes, sugar, salt and bay leaf, breaking up any large chunks of tomato. Simmer 90 minutes, stirring occasionally. Stir in the tomato paste, basil and pepper. Add the meatballs and simmer 30 minutes more. Serve alone or over pasta.

Smoked Beef Tenderloin

 Servings: 8   Cooking Time: 120 Mins.

Ingredients:

- 1 whole beef tenderloin, about 5 lb. (2.3kg) in total, trimmed
- 1/4 C. extra virgin olive oil
- kosher salt and freshly ground black pepper
- 4 garlic cloves, minced
- 1/4 C. chopped fresh basil
- 1/4 C. chopped fresh rosemary
- 1/4 C. chopped fresh oregano
- 1/4 C. chopped fresh marjoram
- 1/4 C. chopped fresh flat-leaf parsley
- 8 hoagie rolls, to serve
- for the sauce
- 2 tbsp mustard seeds
- 1/4 C. Dijon mustard
- 1/4 C. whole grain mustard
- 5 tbsp mayonnaise
- 5 tbsp sour cream
- 2 1/4 tsp Worcestershire sauce
- to smoke
- alder, hickory, or apricot wood chunks

Directions:

1. Rub beef with oil, salt, pepper, garlic, basil, rosemary, oregano, marjoram, and parsley. Wrap tightly with plastic wrap and refrigerate for 4 to 24 hours.
2. To make the sauce, in a medium bowl, combine mustard seeds, Dijon mustard, whole grain mustard, mayonnaise, sour cream, and Worcestershire sauce. Cover the bowl and refrigerate for 1 hour or overnight to allow the flavors to meld.
3. Preheat the grill to 225°F (107°C). Once hot, add the wood chunks and install the heat deflector and a standard grate. Place tenderloin on the grate, close the lid, and smoke until the internal temperature reaches 125°F (52°C), about 1 to 2 hours.
4. Transfer beef to a cutting board and let rest for 15 minutes. While the meat rests, place rolls on the grate cut side down and lightly toast, about 2 to 3 minutes. Thinly slice the meat. To serve, spread the mustard cream sauce on the rolls and pile on the beef.

Mini Lamb Sliders With Tzatziki Sauce

 Servings: 6   Cooking Time: 12 Mins.

Ingredients:

- 1 1/2 lbs ground lamb
- 1 egg
- 2 tsp salt
- 1/2 tsp ground black pepper 2 cloves garlic (chopped)
- 1 tbsp chopped onion
- 1 tsp Italian seasonings
- 1 tsp Worcestershire sauce Mini pita pockets
- Arugula
- 1 C. plain Greek yogurt
- 1 C. sour cream
- 1 C. grated cucumber (peeled and seeded) 1 tsp salt
- 1/4 tsp pepper
- 2 cloves garlic (chopped)
- 2 tbsp lemon juice
- 1 tbsp fresh dill (chopped)
- 1 tsp olive oil
- 1/4 C. light brown sugar
- 1/4 C. brandy
- 1 small container Mascarpone
- 1 tbsp powdered sugar
- 6 slices Angel Food cake
- Maraschino cherries (optional for garnish)

Directions:

1. Preheat the grill to 450°F using direct heat with a cast iron grate installed.
2. Mix first 8 ingredients together and form small patties. Grill sliders in the BGE Slider Basket until done (about 2-3 minutes on each side). Open pita pockets and spoon in some Tzatziki sauce and add arugula. Add lamb sliders and enjoy!
3. Combine all ingredients and mix well. Refrigerate until ready to use.
4. Sprinkle pineapple slices with brown sugar on both sides. Let the slices sit for a few minutes. Grill pineapple for 2-3 minutes on each side or until pineapple slice becomes flexible. Remove from grid and place into a small bowl. Pour brandy on top of the pineapple; cool slightly and cut into quarters.
5. Combine powdered sugar and mascarpone and mix well. In the bottom of a martini glass layer, first the angel food cake, then the mascarpone, then the pineapple. Pour extra sauce into glasses. Garnish with pineapple slices and Maraschino cherries.

Bacon Cheeseburger Hotdogs

 Servings: 8   Cooking Time: 16 Mins.

Ingredients:

- 8 good-quality all-beef hot dogs
- 8 Cobblestone Bread Co.™ Spud Dogs
- drizzle of ketchup
- drizzle of mustard
- chopped fresh parsley
- cheeseburger mixture
- white cheddar cheese sauce
- 6 strips of bacon, diced
- 1 lb. ground beef
- 1-14 ounce can diced tomatoes, drained
- 2 tbsp. ketchup
- 1 tbsp. yellow mustard
- 1 ½ C. grated sharp cheddar cheese, divided
- salt and black pepper
- 2 tbsp. unsalted butter
- 2 tbsp. all-purpose flour
- 1 ½ C. whole milk
- 1 ½ C. grated white cheddar cheese
- pinch of cayenne pepper
- salt and black pepper

Directions:

1. Preheat the grill to 425°F using direct heat with a cast iron grate installed, and add your hot dogs to the grill. Grill for about 2 minutes on each side or until charred and warm. Remove from heat.
2. Assemble your bacon cheeseburger hot dogs, by placing each hot dog on Cobblestone Bread Co.™ Spud Dog. Top with the cheeseburger mixture and spoon the cheese sauce on top. Drizzle with ketchup and yellow mustard. Sprinkle with fresh parsley and the reserved bacon. Enjoy!
3. In a large, nonstick skillet, add the bacon. Fry over medium-low heat until crispy. Transfer the bacon to a plate that has been lined with a paper towel and pour out most of the bacon grease from the skillet. Place it back on the stove, and increase the heat to medium. Add the beef to the pan and cook until brown and cooked through, about 8 minutes. Decrease the heat to low, and add most of the bacon (reserving about 2 tbsp. for garnish) diced tomatoes, ketchup, yellow mustard, cheddar cheese, and salt and black pepper. Stir until the cheese has melted. Cover and keep warm.
4. In a small saucepan, melt the butter for the white cheddar cheese sauce over medium heat. Whisk in the flour and cook for about 1 minute or until golden. Continuing to whisk, add the milk. Cook for about 3-4 minutes or until just slightly thickened. Remove from heat and stir in the white cheddar cheese until melted. Season with a pinch of cayenne pepper and salt and black pepper to taste. Cover and keep warm until you are ready to serve.

POULTRY RECIPES

Grilled Duck Breast With Apple Brandy Glaze

 Servings: 10   Cooking Time: 40 Mins.

Ingredients:

- 4 duck breasts
- 2 tbsp (30 ml) salt
- 2 tbsp (30 ml) black pepper
- 2 tbsp (30 ml) paprika
- 2 chorizo sausage links, meat removed from the casing
- 2 tbsp (30 ml) parsley, chopped
- 3 sage leaves, chopped
- 1½ C. (360 ml) dried cornbread (fresh or bagged)
- ¾ C. (180 ml) chicken stock
- 1½ tbsp (22 ml) extra virgin olive oil
- 1 whole diced shallot or ¼ C. (60 ml) small diced yellow sweet onion
- Salt and pepper, to taste
- ½ C. (120 ml) apple brandy
- 1 C. (240 ml) apple juice
- 2 tbsp (30 ml) sugar
- 1 C. (240 ml) fresh or frozen cranberries
- 1 C. (240 ml) triple sec
- 4 tbsp (60 ml) sugar
- Zest and juice of one medium orange

Directions:

1. Preheat the grill to 375°F using direct heat with a cast iron grate installed.
2. Using a small knife cut a small pocket in each duck breasts, making sure that the pocket goes all the way through the middle of the breast to the other end; do not butterfly the breast. Gently stuff 2 to 4 tbsp (30 to 60 ml) of the chorizo stuffing into each duck breast.
3. Season both sides of the duck with salt, black pepper and paprika. Grill stuffed duck breast, fat side down first, for 8 to 10 minutes on each side until golden brown.
4. Liberally brush glaze on each side of the duck with Apple Brandy Glaze. Let rest on the cutting board for 5 to 7 minutes before cutting; this will allow the juices to distribute evenly and give the duck a resting temperature of 140-145°F for medium doneness. Slice duck breast into ¾ in/2 cm medallions. Serve immediately.
5. Preheat the grill to 350°F using direct heat with a cast iron grate installed.

6. Add olive oil to a Stir-fry & Paella Pan, add chorizo and stir occasionally until cooked through. Add shallot, brown until golden. Add chicken stock and bring to a boil.
7. Remove the Pan from the kamado grill, fold in cornbread, chopped parsley and chopped sage until well incorporated, and cornbread stuffing is moist. Season to taste with salt and pepper. Allow cornbread-sage stuffing to cool before stuffing duck breasts.
8. Pour all ingredients into a Stir-fry & Paella Pan, whisk together and bring to a boil. Reduce heat to 300°F; simmer until sauce forms a glaze consistency, about 20 minutes. Remove glaze from the kamado grill, allow glaze to cool.
9. In a Stir-fry & Paella Pan, combine triple sec, sugar, orange juice and zest; bring to a boil. Add cranberries and cook until cranberries start to pop. Reduce heat to 300°F, until cranberry-orange sauce turns to sauce/glaze consistency; check for desired sauce sweetness at this point.

Green Curry Chicken

 Servings: 4   Cooking Time: 40 Mins.

Ingredients:

- 2 lbs boneless skinless chicken breast, cut into 1 inch cubes
- 1 tbsp. garlic, minced
- 1 tbsp. ginger, grated
- 2 green onions, chopped
- 2 C. unsweetened coconut milk
- 2 tbsp. canola oil
- 2 tbsp. soy sauce
- 2 tbsp. cornstarch
- 2 tbsp. Thai green curry paste
- 2 tbsp. brown sugar
- 1 tbsp. fish sauce

Directions:

1. Preheat the grill to 500°F using direct heat with a cast iron grate installed with the dutch oven on the grid.
2. Dredge chicken breast pieces in soy sauce, then corn starch.
3. Place oil and chicken in the heated dutch oven and brown. Work in batches, being careful not to overcrowd the pan.
4. Add garlic, ginger, and green onion and stir until fragrant.
5. Add Thai green curry paste, fish sauce, coconut milk, and sugar and stir to combine.
6. Lower the temperature in the grill to 350°F.
7. Cover the dutch oven and the dome and simmer for 25-30 minutes.
8. Serve over jasmine rice with lime wedges and whole cilantro leaves.

Blueberry Bbq Chicken

 Servings: 8   Cooking Time: 50 Mins.

Ingredients:

- 1 to 3 lb. (450 g to 1.4 kg) chicken – ask your butcher to butterfly or spatchcock your chicken by cutting the backbone and sternum out and flattening
- 2 tsp (10 ml) salt
- 1½ tsp (8 ml) black pepper
- 3 C. (710 ml) blueberries
- 2 C. (480 ml) apple cider vinegar
- 2 C. (480 ml) granulated sugar
- 1 tsp (5 ml) salt
- One 3-inch cinnamon stick
- 1 bay leaf
- ¼ tsp (2 ml) chili flakes

Directions:

1. 30 minutes before you plan to cook it, bring the chicken to room temperature and season it thoroughly with 2 tsp (10 ml) salt and 1½ tsp (8 ml) black pepper.
2. Preheat the grill to 350°F using direct heat with a cast iron grate installed.
3. Place the chicken skin-side up on the cooking grid and roast for 20 minutes, then begin basting with the blueberry sauce every 5 minutes for an additional 20 minutes of cooking. After 40 minutes total, turn the chicken over to caramelize the skin and baste the other side 10 more minutes. Using a thermometer, check the temperature of the thigh. Once it's at 165°F, remove the chicken from the kamado grill and douse the chicken in blueberry sauce; let rest for 10 minutes, then cut the chicken into 6 or 8 pieces and toss once more in sauce. Serve warm or at room temperature.
4. To make the Blue Q Sauce , begin by combining the blueberries and a little of the vinegar in a food processor. Pulse the berries just to break them up. You're not trying to achieve smooth berries at this point; you just want to get some blue juice flowing. In a dutch oven or 4 quart (3.75 L) saucepan, combine all of the sauce ingredients. Bring to a simmer over medium heat and cook for one hour, covered. Give it a stir from time to time to avoid scorching the bottom.
5. Carefully transfer the sauce to a blender. Pull the little knob off the top of the lid and cover it with a dish towel to prevent a mess! Blend the sauce to get it as smooth as you can, then strain it through a fine mesh strainer and transfer it back to your pan. Cook to reduce it by one-third. The Blue Q should coat the back of a spoon and be the viscosity of maple syrup. Refrigerate overnight to let things mellow out. This sauce will keep for months covered in the refrigerator.

Company Cornish Game Hens

 Servings: 4   Cooking Time: 40 Mins.

Ingredients:

» 4 Cornish Game Hens (about 1 1/4 to 1 1/2 lb. each)
» 1 recipe Lemon Rosemary Marinade

Directions:

1. Pour Lemon Rosemary Marinade over the hens and allow them to marinade for 30 minutes in the refrigerator.
2. Remove from the fridge and allow to come to room temperature while the grill heats.
3. Grilling:
4. Preheat the grill to 450°F using direct heat with a cast iron grate installed.
5. Place the hens on the grid and cover with the dome for 20 minutes.
6. Reduce the heat inside the grill to 350°F and cook for 20 more minutes, or until the internal temperature reaches 165°F.
7. Remove and let rest before serving.

Duck And Mango Quesadilla

 Servings: 24   Cooking Time: 10 Mins.

Ingredients:

- 1 Maple Leaf Farms duck breast*
- 1/2 C. mango, julienne
- 1 tbsp minced green onion
- 1 tbsp minced cilantro
- 1 tbsp sliced jalapenos, seeded
- 4 oz fresh mozzarella, julienne
- 6 flour tortillas, 6"

Directions:

1. Preheat the grill to 350°F using direct heat with a cast iron grate installed.
2. Grill duck breasts on kamado grill for 6 minutes, turning every 2 minutes. Remove skin and shred or cut meat into julienne strips.
3. Evenly divide cheese over bottom half of flour tortillas. Top each evenly with remaining ingredients.
4. Fold each tortilla in half. Gently press down to seal.
5. Grill tortillas on the kamado grill, 2-3 minutes per side until lightly golden.
6. Cut each tortilla into 4 wedges.
7. Roasted Garlic Marinated Duck Breast also works in this recipe.

Paella

 Servings: 6   Cooking Time: 60 Mins.

Ingredients:

- 2 lbs boneless, skinless chicken thighs
- 1 lb. bulk chorizo
- 1 lb. shrimp, peeled and deveined
- 3 cloves garlic, minced
- 2 lemons, zested
- 1 onion, chopped
- 1 bell pepper, chopped
- 1 quart chicken stock
- 2 C. Arborio rice
- 2 tbsp. olive oil
- 1 tbsp. smoked paprika
- 1 tsp dried oregano
- 1/2 tsp salt
- 1/4 tsp crushed red chile flakes

Directions:

1. In a large bowl, combine olive oil, paprika, oregano, salt, and chile flakes
2. Add chicken thighs and stir to combine. Refrigerate while assembling the rest of the ingredients.
3. Grilling:
4. Preheat the grill to 400°F using direct heat with a cast iron grate installed with the dutch oven on the grid.
5. Add chorizo into the dutch oven and cook until browned. Drain all but 2 tbsp. of the fat.
6. Add chicken to the chorizo and brown on both sides.
7. Add onion and bell pepper and cook until vegetables begin to soften.
8. Add rice and garlic and cook for 3 minutes, until the rice begins to toast.
9. Add chicken stock, cover, and lower the dome for 25-30 minutes or until the rice is cooked through.
10. Remove the lid and allow the rice to toast for an additional 5 minutes. Serve.

Tandoori Chicken

 Servings: 4   Cooking Time: 30 Mins.

Ingredients:

- 4 bone-in skinless chicken breasts or thighs
- ½ C. plain Greek yogurt
- 1 lime, juiced
- 1 tbsp garam masala
- 4 cloves garlic, finely grated
- 1 inch of fresh ginger, finely grated
- ½ tbsp dry ginger powder
- ½ tbsp red chili powder
- ¼ tbsp cayenne pepper
- ½ tsp ground nutmeg
- ½ tbsp crushed fenugreek leaves
- ½ tbsp salt
- ¼ tsp red food color (Optional)

Directions:

1. One day before cooking, add all ingredients except the chicken in a bowl, and stir until combined. Make deep slashes in chicken and pour marinade over top. Massage the chicken to ensure all sides are coated. Marinade in the fridge for the flavors to deepen.
2. Preheat the grill to 400°F using direct heat with a cast iron grate installed.
3. Place Chicken onto the grill, bone side down. Cook for approximately 15 minutes per side or until chicken reaches and internal temperature of 165°F.
4. Serve with sweet white onions, warm naan and basmati rice.

Braised Chicken Thighs With Mushrooms

 Servings: 4   Cooking Time: 60 Mins.

Ingredients:

- 2 lbs chicken thighs, bone in and skin on
- 1 lb. mushrooms, thinly sliced
- 1 C. finely chopped onion
- 1 tbsp. butter
- 1 tbsp. fresh thyme, chopped
- 1/2 C. white wine
- 1/2 C. chicken broth
- 1/4 C. flour
- 2 tbsp. olive oil
- Salt and Pepper

Directions:

1. Lightly dredge each chicken thigh in flour and season with salt and pepper.
2. Preheat the grill to 500°F using direct heat with a cast iron grate installed.
3. Place the dutch oven directly on the grid and allow the pot to heat for 5-7 minutes.
4. Pour olive oil into the oven and add chicken thighs, being careful not to crowd the pan.
5. Brown the chicken thighs in batches until they are golden brown on all sides. Remove from the dutch oven and set aside.
6. To the pan, add butter and mushrooms, but do not stir for 2-3 minutes or until the mushrooms begin to brown.
7. Add onions and cook until softened.
8. Return the chicken to the pot and add wine, chicken, broth, and thyme.
9. Cover the dutch oven, reduce the heat of The grill to 350°F and close the dome.
10. Allow the chicken to cook 30-40 minutes or until the internal temperature reaches 170°F. Serve warm.

Chicken Keema Burgers

 Servings: 4   **Cooking Time: 12 Mins.**

Ingredients:

- 2 lbs ground chicken
- 1/2 C. fresh breadcrumbs
- 1 tbsp. olive oil
- 2 cloves garlic, finely chopped
- 1 small onion, finely chopped
- 1 egg
- 4 pieces Naan
- 2 tbsp. Indian Spice Rub
- 1/2 C. Greek style yogurt
- 1/2 C. finely chopped, seeded, cucumber
- 2 tbsp. chopped fresh cilantro
- 1 tsp finely chopped green onion
- 1/4 tsp ground cumin

Directions:

1. In a small bowl, combine ingredients for the raita and set aside. The raita can be made a day in advance, covered, and refrigerated.
2. In a small skillet, heat olive oil over medium and add onion and garlic. Cook until soft and translucent. Set aside to cool.
3. In a medium bowl, combine ground chicken, bread crumbs, onion mixture, egg, and Indian Spice Rub until combined. Form 4 patties and return to the fridge to chill for 10 minutes.
4. Grilling:
5. Preheat the grill to 500°F using direct heat with a cast iron grate installed.
6. Place burgers on the grid and close the dome for 3 minutes.
7. Flip burgers and close the dome for 3 more minutes.
8. Close all of the vents and allow the burgers to sit for 5-6 minutes or until the internal temperature reaches 170°F.
9. Serve burgers on naan, topped with raita.

Country Chicken Saltimbocca

 Servings: 8   Cooking Time: 30 Mins.

Ingredients:

- 3 6-8 oz (170-225 g) chicken breasts
- 4 C. (960 ml) cleaned and destemmed collard greens
- 6 slices cooked Applewood-smoked bacon, crumbled
- 2 tbsp (30 ml) extra virgin olive oil
- 2 cloves garlic, minced
- 3 slices aged cheddar cheese
- 1 tbsp (15 ml) garlic powder
- 1 tbsp (15 ml) onion powder
- 1 tsp (5 ml) white pepper
- 1 tbsp (15 ml) seasoning salt
- 4 tbsp (60 ml) butter
- 4 tbsp (60 ml) flour
- 2 C. (480 ml) half-and-half
- Reserved liquid from chicken
- 1 tbsp (15 ml) smoked paprika
- 6 leaves of basil

Directions:

1. Preheat the grill to 350°F using direct heat with a cast iron grate installed.
2. Pound chicken breasts until ¼ inch thick. Coat chicken breasts with ¾ of the seasoning mix; set aside.
3. Chiffonade collard greens into strips no wider than ¼ inch. Heat a Cast Iron Skillet with the olive oil. Add greens, then garlic and the remaining seasoning mix, cooking until wilted, 5-7 minutes.
4. Lay out the chicken breasts with the interior side up. Layer each in the following order: one slice of cheese, 1/3 of the bacon crumbles, 1/3 of the cooked collards. The bacon and collards should be placed in a thin even layer across the whole breast. Beginning at the short tapered end, roll up each chicken breast as you would for a jellyroll. Secure with a toothpick.
5. Place rolls in a Roasting & Drip Pan, evenly spaced with room between each roll.
6. Place the pan on the grid and bake for 15 to 20 minutes or until the chicken is firm. Remove from the kamado grill and allow to rest for at least 5 minutes. Remove the chicken from the pan; reserve the liquid for the sauce.
7. Remove the platesetter and grill each side of the chicken for 1 minute for color and added flavor. Gently slice each into pinwheels, no less than ½ inch wide. Top with sauce and serve.
8. Mix all seasoning ingredients together and set aside.
9. Melt butter in a sauce pan. Whisk flour into butter. Cook for 90 seconds once incorporated, continuously whisking. Slowly add half-and-half, whisking in each addition until incorporated in flour mix. Season to taste. Add the reserved chicken liquid the same way. Add smoked paprika and cook at a low simmer for 2 minutes, or until it's at the thickness you desire; remove from heat. Chiffonade basil, add to warm sauce just before serving.

Spatchcocked Chicken Two Ways

 Servings: 4   Cooking Time: 100 Mins.

Ingredients:

- 2 quarts hot water
- 1 C. kosher salt
- 1⅓ C. Sugar in The Raw
- ¼ C. powdered onion
- ¼ C. granulated garlic
- 2 tbsp black pepper
- Ice, enough to bring brine to 1 gallon
- 1 whole chicken about 4 lb. each, cut spatchcock style
- Nashville Hot Seasoning
- 1 whole chicken about 4 lb. each, cut spatchcock style
- Citrus & Herb Seasoning

Directions:

1. One day before the cook, make the brine. In a deep container, combine the water, salt, sugar, granulated onion, granulated garlic, and pepper. Mix well until the salt and sugar are dissolved. Pour the ice into the bowl with the hot brine. Mix well. When the brine has completely cooled, place in the refrigerator for at least 4 hours until well chilled. Use immediately or keep refrigerated for up to a week.
2. At least 12 hours and up to 24 hours before you plan to cook, put the chicken in the brine and weigh it down to keep it completely submerged. Refrigerate until needed.
3. Preheat the grill to 400°F using direct heat with a cast iron grate installed.
4. Remove the chicken from the brine. Rinse thoroughly and dry well with paper towels. Season the chicken on all sides with the Nashville Hot Seasoning.
5. Place the chicken on the cooking grid – meaty side up – and cook for about 15 minutes until well browned on the bottom. Flip the chicken and cook until golden brown on the skin side, about 15 minutes. Flip the chicken again and cook until it reaches an internal temperature of 165°F deep in the breast and 180°F in the thigh. Remove to a platter and tent loosely with foil. Let rest for 5 minutes. Carve to serve.
6. Preheat the grill to 350°F using direct heat with a cast iron grate installed.
7. Remove the chicken from the brine. Rinse thoroughly and dry well with paper towels. Season the chicken on all sides with the Citrus & Herb Seasoning.
8. Place the chicken on the cooking grid meaty side up and cook for about 1 hour and 15 minutes until golden brown and cooked to an internal temperature of 165°F deep in the breast and 180°F in the thigh. Remove to a platter and tent loosely with foil. Let rest for 5 minutes. Carve to serve.

PORK RECIPES

Blt Soup

 Servings: 4   Cooking Time: 4 Mins.

Ingredients:

- 8 slices bacon, crisply-cooked
- 1 28- oz can crushed tomatoes
- 14½ oz can chicken broth
- 15 oz can white beans (cannellini or navy)
- 1½ tsp. Italian seasoning
- 2 tsp. balsamic vinegar
- 1 C. leaf lettuce, shredded
- ¼ C. fresh basil, thinly sliced

Directions:

1. Preheat the grill to 450°F using direct heat with a cast iron grate installed.
2. Coarsely crumble bacon and set aside. In dutch oven, stir together tomatoes, broth, beans and seasoning. Bring to a simmer; stir in vinegar. In small bowl, toss together lettuce and basil. Ladle soup into large soup plates or bowls; garnish each serving with crumbled bacon and lettuce and basil.

Prosciutto Wrapped Cheese Dogs

 Servings: 6   Cooking Time: 12 Mins.

Ingredients:

- 6 Nature's Own 100% Whole Wheat Hot Dog Rolls
- 1 tsp. Italian seasoning
- 3 pieces string cheese
- 6 prosciutto slices
- 2 tsp. olive oil
- 6 fat-free hot dogs
- Dijon mustard
- Chopped tomato

Directions:

1. Preheat the grill to 375°F using direct heat with a cast iron grate installed.
2. Cut a lengthwise slit down center of each hot dog; do not cut all the way through bottom or ends. Sprinkle Italian seasoning evenly over hot dogs, rolling to coat.
3. Pull each string cheese piece in half vertically, forming 6 pieces. Stuff 1 cheese piece into each hot dog slit. Wrap 1 prosciutto slice around each stuffed hot dog, encasing completely. Brush prosciutto lightly with oil. Place hot dogs on baking sheet.
4. Cook 10 to 12 minutes or until heated through and cheese melts. Place hot dogs in rolls. Top with mustard, tomato and basil.

Duck & Potatoes

 Servings: 12   Cooking Time: 90 Mins.

Ingredients:

- 8 duck breasts, about 4 lb. (1.8kg) in total
- 8 mild green chile peppers
- 4 tbsp olive oil
- kosher salt and freshly ground black pepper
- 1 large white onion, chopped
- 1 tbsp cumin seeds
- 15 tomatillos, husked, rinsed, and cut into wedges
- 1 C. chicken stock
- 2 tsp dried oregano
- 1 lb. (450g) Yukon Gold potatoes, peeled and cut into cubes
- chopped fresh cilantro, to garnish
- for the brine
- 1/2 C. kosher salt
- 1/2 C. packed light brown sugar
- 3 tbsp pickling spice
- 6 C. hot water
- for the salsa verde
- 2 C. chicken stock
- 5 tomatillos, husked, rinsed, and cut into wedges
- 1 bunch of scallions, coarsely chopped
- 1 1/2 C. packed fresh cilantro leaves and tender stems
- 6 garlic cloves, peeled

Directions:

1. To make the brine, in a medium bowl, whisk together salt, brown sugar, pickling spice, and water until salt and sugar have dissolved. Add ice cubes a few at a time until the liquid is no longer hot. Place duck breasts in a resealable plastic bag and add brine to cover. (Any extra brine can be refrigerated and saved for a later use.) Refrigerate for 1 hour.

2. Preheat the grill to 350°F (177°C) using direct heat with a cast iron grate installed and a dutch oven on the grate. Place green chiles on the grate around the dutch oven, close the grill lid, and grill until charred, about 7 to 10 minutes. Remove from the grill, seed, dice, and set aside.

3. In the hot dutch oven, heat oil until shimmering. Remove duck from the brine, pat dry with paper towels, and slice into thin strips. Sprinkle duck with salt and pepper to taste. Working in two batches, add duck to the dutch

oven. Leave the lid off the dutch oven, close the grill lid, and cook until browned, about 4 minutes per batch, turning occasionally. Using a slotted spoon, transfer duck to a serving bowl, retaining 1 tbsp fat.
4. Add onion to the dutch oven and sauté until soft, about 5 minutes. Add cumin seeds and cook until onion is golden and cumin is toasted, about 2 minutes. Add tomatillos and cook until tender and browned in spots, about 8 minutes, stirring occasionally.
5. To make the salsa verde, in a blender or food processor, purée all the salsa ingredients until smooth. Return duck and any juices to the dutch oven. Add 2 C. salsa verde, chicken stock, chiles, and oregano. Place the lid on the dutch oven, close the grill lid, and simmer until duck is tender, about 2 hours.
6. Add potatoes to the dutch oven. Replace the lid, close the grill lid, and simmer until potatoes are tender, about 30 minutes. Stir in remaining salsa verde and bring to a simmer. Thin with more stock (if desired), and season with salt and pepper to taste. Sprinkle with cilantro before serving.

Pork Tortas Ahogada

Servings: 12 **Cooking Time: 240 Mins.**

Ingredients:

- 16 garlic cloves, minced
- 2 tbsp fresh oregano, minced
- 1/4 C. kosher salt, plus more as needed
- 1/4 ground black pepper, plus more as needed
- 9 lb. (4.1kg) boneless pork butt
- 12 hoagie buns
- for the sauce
- 6 tbsp vegetable oil
- 4 medium white onions, chopped
- 8 garlic cloves, minced
- 4 x 28 oz (794g) cans whole peeled tomatoes
- 8 chipotle peppers in adobo
- 5 tsp dried oregano
- 1 1/2 tsp kosher salt
- 1/4 tsp sugar
- to smoke
- grapevine, peach, or oak wood chunks

Directions:

1. In a small bowl, combine garlic, oregano, salt, and pepper. Use a sharp knife to make 1-in (2.5-cm) cuts all over pork. Fill the cuts with the garlic mixture, and rub the exterior of the meat with more salt and pepper to taste.
2. Preheat the grill to 350°F (177°C). Once hot, add the wood chunks and install the heat deflector and a standard grate. Place pork in a shallow roasting pan (a disposable aluminum pan works well) and place the pan on the grate. Close the lid and roast until pork is tender, cooked through, and reaches an internal temperature of 190°F (88°C), about 2 to 3 hours. Remove pork from the grill and let rest for 20 minutes before slicing thinly, reserving the pan drippings.
3. To make the sauce, in a large pot on the stovetop over high heat, heat oil until almost smoking. Add onion and garlic, lower the heat to medium-high, and sauté until onion is translucent, about 2 to 3 minutes. Add the reserved pan drippings, tomatoes, peppers, oregano, salt, and sugar, and lower the heat to a simmer. Cook uncovered until the sauce is hot and the vegetables begin to soften, about 10 to 15 minutes, stirring frequently. Using an immersion blender, purée the sauce, then strain through a mesh sieve, using a spoon to press the liquid through.
4. Slice rolls in half lengthwise, removing some of the insides. Spoon 2 tbsp chipotle sauce over each half, top with the sliced pork, then spoon 1/4 C. sauce over each torta. Place tortas in a clean roasting pan and return to the grill until heated through, about 2 to 3 minutes. Serve immediately with any remaining sauce.

Takeo Spikes' Ribs

Servings: 4 **Cooking Time: 130 Mins.**

Ingredients:

- Ribs
- Your favorite BBQ Rub
- Yellow mustard
- Apple juice

Directions:

1. Take ribs out of the fridge and begin prep work. This will take about 30 minutes to an hour.
2. Remove the membrane, which is a thick plastic-like skin over the boney part of the ribs. Removing this allows the smoke to penetrate the meat better. Pry up on the membrane using a knife or other sharp utensil. Then grab the membrane with a paper towel and pull it clean off.
3. Then I apply a light coating of yellow hot dog mustard to the bony side of the ribs to help the rub to stick real good. Once the bony or bottom side of the ribs are coated with mustard and rub. I flip them over and do the same with the top side. Light coat of mustard then sprinkle on the rub. Not too thick but enough to cover the ribs real good. Once the ribs are coated on both sides with rub and mustard, I leave them there to go get the kamado grill ready.
4. Make sure you have plenty of lump charcoal in the fire bowl. I like to have it up to the top of the bowl, which is an inch or two above the air holes. Place the platesetter in place with the legs facing up then place the grate on top of that. If you are worried about the drippings on your platesetter, you can place a drip pan on it or some foil which can be easily thrown away when you're finished cooking.
5. After the coals have been burning for about 7 minutes, close the dome and leave the bottom and top vents all the way open until the kamado grill reaches about 230°F. While the kamado grill is heating up, go ahead and get the ribs and place them on the grate bone side down.
6. Once the kamado grill reaches 230°F, adjust the vent at the bottom and the top to hold this temperature. For me, that means the daisy wheel at the top is only slightly cracked open at about 20% open and the bottom vent is open about ¾ of an inch or so.
7. This is where the 2-2-1 method of making the ribs tender really starts. Start a timer or just make note of the time because the ribs will only stay in this current configuration for 2 hours.
8. Once 2 hours are up, the ribs should be wrapped in heavy duty foil or an easier method is to place them in a large foil pan with foil covering the top tightly. Then place back on the grill. Some folks put (only a little) apple juice down in the pan to create more steam and flavors. It is this steaming action that super tenderizes the ribs.
9. This is the 2nd step in the 2-2-1 method and lasts 2 hours, just like the first step. After 2 hours have expired with the ribs in foil or in the covered pan, remove them from the pan or foil and place them once again directly on the grates for 1 hour.
10. When they come out of the foil or pan, they look wet and there is no crust to speak of. The last hour on the grates dries the top a little and develops the crust on the outside that is usually desired. This is the last step and when the hour is up, the ribs are ready to slice and eat.
11. You will pull them off at 185-190°F internal temp in between the bones.

Christmas Gingersnap Ham

Servings: 15 **Cooking Time:** 90 Mins.

Ingredients:

- 1 (8-10 pound) spiral sliced ham
- 2 C. gingersnap cookies, crushed
- 1/4 C. brown mustard

Directions:

1. Remove the ham from its wrapper, thoroughly rinse it and pat it dry.
2. Place the ham in a heat-proof roasting pan.
3. Brush the outside liberally with mustard.
4. Press the gingersnap cookies into the mustard coating.
5. Grilling:
6. Preheat the grill to 350°F using direct heat with a cast iron grate installed.
7. Place the ham inside the grill and close the dome for 1 to 1 1/2 hours.
8. Allow the ham to rest for 20 minutes before carving and serving.

The Perfect Gift For Your Favorite Egghead

Servings: 4 **Cooking Time: 75 Mins.**

Ingredients:

- 2 slabs St. Louis–style pork spareribs, about 4 lb. total
- 1/4 C. apple juice
- 1/4 C. cider vinegar
- 1/4 C. paprika
- 3 tbsp. raw sugar
- 2 tbsp. kosher salt
- 1 tbsp. granulated onion
- 1 tbsp. granulated garlic
- 1 tsp. dried basil leaves
- 1 tsp. cayenne pepper

Directions:

1. Preheat the grill to 300°F using direct heat with a cast iron grate installed. To make the rub, combine all of the ingredients in a small bowl and mix well. Peel the membrane off the back of each slab of ribs. Season the ribs on both sides using about half of the rub. Let the ribs rest for 15 minutes, or until the rub is tacky.
2. Lay the ribs, meaty side up, on the kamado grill cooking grid and cook for 2 hours. Flip the ribs and cook for 1 hour longer, or until the ribs are nicely browned on both sides.
3. Lay 2 big doubled sheets of heavy-duty aluminum foil on a work surface. Lay a rib slab, meaty side up, on the center of each doubled foil stack. In a small bowl, stir together the apple juice and vinegar, mixing well. Fold up the edges of each foil stack and then add 1/4 C. of the juice mixture to each packet. Close up each rib packet snugly, being careful not to puncture the foil with a rib bone. Reserve the remaining 1/2 C. juice mixture.
4. Put the ribs back in the kamado grill and cook for 1 hour, or until tender when poked with a toothpick or fork. Remove the ribs from the foil packets and place them, bone side down, on the grid. Drizzle the ribs with 1/3 C. of the reserved juice mixture and sprinkle them with some of the remaining rub. Cook for about another 15 minutes, or until the ribs are dry.
5. Transfer to a platter and drizzle with the remaining juice mixture. With a big knife, cut the ribs into individual bones. Serve with any remaining rub on the side.

Barbecued Pork Shoulder With Carolina Sauce

Servings: 12 **Cooking Time: 660 Mins.**

Ingredients:

- 1 whole bone in pork butt, about 8 pounds
- 2 tbsp olive oil
- Savory Pecan Seasoning
- 1/2 C. apple juice
- Bold and Tangy Carolina Barbecue Sauce

Directions:

1. Preheat the grill to 275°F using direct heat with a cast iron grate installed.
2. Trim any loose fat from the butt but leave the heavy fat cap on. Rub the butt all over with the oil and season the butt liberally on all the meaty surfaces with the Savory Pecan Seasoning.
3. Place the butt on the kamado grill fat side down. Cook for about 8 hours until it reaches an internal temperature of 170°. Lay out a big sheet of double thick heavy-duty aluminum foil and put the pork butt in the middle. fat side up. As you begin to close up the package pour the apple juice in the bottom and then seal the package. Put the butt back in the kamado grill and cook until it reaches an internal temperature of 200° deep in the meaty part. This should take another 2 to 3 hours.
4. When the pork is done remove it from the kamado grill and open the package. Let cool for 15 minutes. With meat claws pull the pork apart discarding any fat or bones. Top it with the Bold and Tangy Carolina Barbecue Sauce or Vidalia Onion Sriracha Barbecue Sauce and toss to combine. Serve with sauce on the side.

Pulled Pork Sandwiches

Servings: 12 **Cooking Time:** 480 Mins.

Ingredients:

- One 7 to 8 lb. pork butt, fat cap trimmed off
- 2 tbsp. vegetable oil
- Big Time BBQ Rub
- ½ C. apple juice
- 2 C. Dr. BBQ's Carolina Barbecue sauce
- 12 hamburger buns
- ½ C. salt
- ½ C. turbinado sugar
- ¼ C. granulated brown sugar
- 1 tbsp. granulated garlic
- 1 tbsp. granulated onion
- 2 tbsp. paprika
- 2 tbsp. chili powder
- 2 tbsp. freshly ground black pepper
- 2 tsp. cayenne
- 1 tbsp. thyme leaves
- 1 tbsp. ground cumin
- 1 tsp. ground nutmeg
- 1 c vinegar
- 2/3 C. catsup
- 2 tsp. sugar
- 1 tsp. salt
- 1 tsp. Worcestershire
- ½ tsp. red pepper flakes

Directions:

1. Rub the meat with the oil and then sprinkle liberally with the rub. Put in the refrigerator for at least a half hour and up to 12 hours.
2. Preheat the grill to 275°F using direct heat with a cast iron grate installed. Put the butt in the kamado grill and cook until the internal temperature is 160°F; this should take 6 to 8 hours. Lay out a big double piece of heavy duty aluminum foil and put the pork butt in the middle. As you begin to close up the package pour the apple juice over the top of the butt and then seal the package, taking care not to puncture it put it back in the kamado grill and cook until the meat reaches an internal temperature of 195°F; this should take another 2 to 3 hours.
3. Remove the package from the kamado grill to a baking sheet. Open the top of the foil to let the steam out and let it rest for ½ hour. Using heavy neoprene gloves or a pair of tongs and a fork transfer the meat to a big pan. It will be very tender and hard to handle. Discard the juices as they will be quite fatty. Shred the meat, discarding the fat and bones; it should just fall apart. Continue to pull the meat until it's shredded enough to make a sandwich. Add 1 C. of the sauce and mix well. Reserve the additional sauce for serving on the side. Serve on fluffy white buns topped with cole slaw.
4. Combine all ingredients, mix well, and store in an airtight container.
5. In a small saucepan mix together the vinegar, catsup, sugar, salt, Worcestershire and pepper flakes. Cook over low heat for 5 minutes stirring to blend.

Bacon-wrapped Pig Wings

Servings: 12 **Cooking Time: 90 Mins.**

Ingredients:

- 4 one-inch thick boneless pork chops
- 12 slices of bacon (do not used thick sliced)
- Barbecue rub
- Barbecue sauce

Directions:

1. Preheat the grill to 235°F using direct heat with a cast iron grate installed.
2. Cut each pork chop into three strips. To wrap the "wings" start by overlapping the bacon on one end of a pork strip, then wrapping it up and around in a candy-cane fashion. Secure the bacon at the top with a toothpick. Season the bacon-wrapped wings liberally with the rub. Place wings directly on the cooking grid and cook for 90 minutes, or until the bacon is cooked. Serve hot with barbecue sauce for dipping.

Leg Of Warthog

Servings: 8 **Cooking Time: 240 Mins.**

Ingredients:

- 1 Leg of warthog (if warthog is unavailable, substitute pork loin or wild boar)
- 1 lb. (450 g) streaky bacon
- 2 tsp (10 ml) mixture of garlic and herb seasonings
- 1 tsp (5 ml) ground cloves
- 1 C. (250 ml) vegetable stock powder
- 2 tsp (10 ml) ground ginger
- Healthy splash of white wine
- 1 C. (250 ml) apricot jam
- Zest of 1 naartjie (or tangerine)
- ½ C. (125 ml) olive oil
- Salt and black pepper to taste
- 4 C. (1 liter) water
- 1 lemon
- 1 large carrot, chopped
- 1 celery stick, chopped
- 4 whole chili peppers

Directions:

1. Roll the bacon in the garlic and herb seasonings. Lard the warthog leg first with a piece of naartjie peel and then with the seasoned bacon. Keep bacon in place with toothpicks.
2. Mix the remainder of the dry ingredients and wet ingredients together to make the marinade. Experiment and add whatever you like from the cupboard. The marinade needs to be sweet and sticky. In South Africa, this is called "sommer gooi" cooking ("just throw").
3. Place the leg in a Dutch Oven, add marinade and cover. Marinate for 24 hours in the refrigerator.
4. Preheat the grill to 300°F using direct heat with a cast iron grate installed.
5. Add extra water, carrots, quartered lemon, celery and chili peppers to the Dutch Oven.
6. Cover and cook slowly for about 4 hours. Baste the leg from time to time and check to make sure leg is still sitting in at least 1 to 2 inches (2.5 to 5 cm) of liquid.
7. Remove leg from Dutch Oven, place on the cooking grid and cook for another hour, basting regularly. When done, the meat should be easily coming off the bone and should fall apart.
8. Allow to rest for 10 minutes before serving.
9. While the meat is resting, use the leftover juices in the Dutch Oven to make gravy. The gravy should be sweet with a slight chili bite. Add extra apricot jam and chilis if necessary.
10. Serve with chili steamed cabbage and garlic mashed potatoes.

FISH AND SEAFOOD RECIPES

Grilled Oysters

Servings: 2 **Cooking Time: 5 Mins.**

Ingredients:

- A dozen fresh oysters (the fresher, closer-to-home you can get the better!)
- 6 Tbsp – a little more than half a package – slow-cultured, Roasted Garlic Basil & Parsley Banner Butter
- 1 lemon, cut into slices or wedges
- 3 Tbsp fresh chives, roughly chopped

Directions:

1. Preheat the grill to 425°F using direct heat with a cast iron grate installed.
2. Take your Roasted Garlic Basil & Parsley Banner Butter out of the fridge and set aside in a small bowl.
3. Carefully shuck the oysters with a small knife (an oyster knife with a rounded tip and a work glove on the hand grasping the oyster is a good choice for novice shuckers). Remove the top, flat shell and discard. Place the rounded (bowl side of the shell) side with the oyster on a Perforated Cooking Grid.
4. Place the Perforated Grid in the kamado grill and then add a half tbsp. of softened Roasted Garlic butter to each oyster.
5. Close the lid and kamado grill for 4 or 5 minutes until the oysters are bubbling (not rubbery). The butter should be completely melted and beginning to caramelize on the shell when done.
6. Remove from the kamado grill and move the oysters to a serving plate with the lemons. Squeeze a few wedges/slices onto the oysters and then scatter the chives across the plate.

Grilled Asian Mahi-mahi

Servings: 4   **Cooking Time:** 24 Mins.

Ingredients:

- 4 (1 inch thick) Mahi-Mahi filets
- 1 tbsp. Better Than Bouillon Fish Base
- 1/2 C. soy sauce
- 1 1/2 tbsp. sesame oil
- 1 tsp. honey
- 1/2 tsp. garlic powder
- 2 tsp. sesame seeds

Directions:

1. Preheat the grill to 400°F using direct heat with a cast iron grate installed.
2. Mix the fish base, soy sauce, sesame oil, honey and garlic powder in a medium-sized shallow bowl. Add the Mahi-Mahi to the bowl and marinate for 20 minutes.
3. Place the Mahi-Mahi directly onto the kamado grill and grill for 3-4 minutes per side.
4. Remove the fish from the grill, sprinkle with the sesame seeds and serve immediately.

Smoked King Salmon

Servings: 8 **Cooking Time: 75 Mins.**

Ingredients:

- 2 lb. (1kg) skinless King salmon fillets
- for the brine
- 1/2 C. kosher salt
- 1/2 C. packed light brown sugar
- 3 tbsp pickling spice
- 6 C. hot water
- for the pesto
- 5 tbsp extra virgin olive oil, divided
- 1/4 C. walnut halves
- 2 C. baby arugula, loosely packed
- 1 C. fresh basil leaves, loosely packed
- 3 tbsp freshly grated Parmigiano-Reggiano
- 1 garlic clove
- kosher salt and freshly ground black pepper
- to smoke
- alder or cedar wood chunks

Directions:

1. To make the brine, in a medium bowl, whisk together salt, brown sugar, pickling spice, and water until salt and sugar have dissolved. Add ice cubes until the liquid is no longer hot. Place salmon in a resealable plastic bag, add the brine to cover, and refrigerate for 30 minutes. (Any extra brine can be refrigerated and saved for a later use.)

2. Remove salmon from the brine, pat dry with paper towels, and refrigerate until the surface begins to look dry and feel slightly tacky, about 30 to 60 minutes more.

3. Preheat the grill to 225°F (107°C) using indirect heat. Once hot, add the wood chunks and install a cast iron grate and a cast iron skillet. Place 1 tbsp oil and walnuts in the skillet, close the lid, and cook until they just begin to toast, about 10 to 15 minutes. Remove the walnuts from the grill and let cool.

4. To make the pesto, in a food processor, combine walnuts, arugula, basil, Parmigiano-Reggiano, and garlic. Process until the mixture is finely chopped. With the processor running, slowly add 4 tbsp oil until well combined. Thin the pesto with 1 tbsp water (if desired). Transfer to a bowl and season with salt and pepper to taste.

5. Place salmon on the grate, close the lid, and cook until the fish reaches an internal temperature of 135°F (57°C) and just begins to flake, about 45 to 60 minutes. Remove salmon from the grill, and serve immediately with the pesto.

Grilled Fish Tacos With Peach Salsa

Servings: 4 **Cooking Time: 10 Mins.**

Ingredients:

- 1 tsp. cumin
- 1 tsp. brown sugar
- 1 tsp. ground coriander
- 2 tsp. olive oil
- 1½ lb. fresh salmon, halibut, catfish, or your favorite fish
- Corn tortillas
- Lime wedges
- 1½ C. diced fresh peaches
- 1 firm, but ripe avocado, diced
- ¼ C. thinly sliced red onion
- 2 tbsp. chopped fresh cilantro
- ½ small jalapeño, minced
- juice of 1 lime, about 3 tablespoons

Directions:

1. Preheat the grill to 400°F using direct heat with a cast iron grate installed.
2. In a small bowl, combine cumin, sugar, and coriander. Brush fish with olive oil and sprinkle with spice mixture. Grill fish on oiled cooking grid for 3-5 minutes per side until cooked to your liking. Char tortillas on cooking grid, about 10 seconds on each side.
3. Serve tacos with fresh salsa and desired toppings. (cheese, etc.)
4. Combine salsa ingredients in a medium bowl and refrigerate until ready to use.

Arctic Char With Blood Orange Salad

Servings: 2   **Cooking Time: 10 Mins.**

Ingredients:

- 1 filet of arctic char
- 1 lemon, zested
- Salt to taste
- ½ bunch of parsley, picked
- Supremes of 3 blood oranges
- 2 tbsp of olive oil
- 1 radish, sliced
- Salt to taste
- ½ bunch parsley, chopped
- 2 serrano peppers, chopped
- ½ C. of olive oil
- 3 tsp white balsamic vinegar
- 2 cloves garlic, roasted
- 1 lemon, juiced and zested

Directions:

1. Preheat the grill to 400°F using direct heat with a cast iron grate installed.
2. Add the lemon zest to both sides of the arctic char and set aside.
3. Lightly oil the cast iron grate with a basting brush. Remove any excess moisture on the arctic char's skin with a paper towel and add the salt. Cook the fish skin side down for 5 minutes. Flip and cook for another 3-5 minutes. While the fish is cooking prepare your plate by spreading the lemon and herb sauce liberally on the plate. Remove the char from the kamado grill and place the fish flesh side down on the sauce.
4. Serve immediately with the blood orange salad.
5. Mix together all the ingredients for the blood orange salad and set aside.
6. Mix together all the ingredients for the lemon and herb sauce and set aside.

Maple-glazed Applewood Smoked Octopus

Servings: 4　　　**Cooking Time: 30 Mins.**

Ingredients:

- Sushi grade, precooked, octopus tentacles
- 100% Canadian maple syrup

Directions:

1. Defrost the octopus and bring to room temperature.
2. Preheat the grill to 225°F using direct heat with a cast iron grate installed.
3. Place octopus tentacles on the indirect side of grill. Make sure your grid has been cleaned and seasoned with oil as to not tear the octopus while grilling.
4. After a few minutes, start to glaze the octopus tentacles with real 100% Canadian maple syrup. Continue to glaze every five minutes for the next half hour.
5. Remove the octopus from the grill and place onto a plate and open vents fully and open the lid of the kamado grill. Once the coals are red on the direct side, place the octopus on a clean oil-seasoned grill and glaze again.
6. After a minute or less, depending how it's cooking, you will want to flip and glaze the tentacles again. You don't want it so hot that the suction C. fall off, once they start to blacken it's time to flip them one last time with another glaze. Remove the tentacles to a platter and let rest for five minutes.
7. Slice tentacles into ½ inch thick pieces, drizzle one last time with maple syrup and serve. I prefer Kewpie Japanese Mayo, Kentucky Bourbon Barbecue Sauce or Hoison sauce for dipping.

Raspberry Glazed Salmon

Servings: 4 **Cooking Time: 28 Mins.**

Ingredients:

» Cedar grilling plank
» Fresh salmon fillet
» Raspberry BBQ Sauce

Directions:

1. Place the cedar plank in a pan, cover with water and soak for 2 hours. Coat salmon with raspberry BBQ sauce and let marinate for 2 hours.
2. Preheat the grill to 350°F using direct heat with a cast iron grate installed.
3. Place plank on cooking grid, close the dome and heat for about 3 minutes. Flip plank, using tongs, and place salmon on heated side of plank. Close dome and cook for 20-25 minutes.

Swordfish Steaks With Peach Salsa

Servings: 4 **Cooking Time: 15 Mins.**

Ingredients:

- 4 swordfish steaks (about 1 inch thick, or 6 ounces)
- 1 tbsp. olive oil
- Salt & Pepper
- 1/4 C. finely diced red pell pepper
- 1 tbsp. olive oil
- 1/4 tsp cumin
- 2 peaches, slightly underripe, diced
- 1 jalapeño, seeded and finely chopped
- The juice and zest of 1 lime

Directions:

1. Combine ingredients for the salsa and set aside.
2. Brush both sides of the swordfish steaks with olive oil and season with salt and pepper.
3. Grilling:
4. Preheat the grill to 400°F using direct heat with a cast iron grate installed.
5. Place the steaks directly on the grid and close the dome for 6 minutes.
6. Gently flip the fish and close the dome for another 6-8 minutes or until the fish is firm.
7. Remove from the grid and serve topped with peach salsa.

Seared Tuna

Servings: 6 **Cooking Time: 2 Mins.**

Ingredients:

- 8 oz filet ahi tuna steak
- 1 tsp salt
- 1 tsp pepper
- 1 tsp wasabi powder
- Multicolored sesame seeds
- 2 tbsp avocado oil

Directions:

1. Preheat the grill to 450°F using direct heat with a cast iron grate installed.
2. Season the tuna with the salt, pepper and wasabi powder. Then coat the tuna in sesame seeds.
3. Coat the plancha with the avocado oil and place the steaks on the plancha. Sear for 30 to 40 seconds per side. Remove from the kamado grill and slice to your preference, we suggest ¼ to ½ inch thick. Serve immediately over sautéed zucchini noodles or a lightly dressed salad.

Miso Poached Sea Bass

Servings: 4   **Cooking Time:** 55 Mins.

Ingredients:

- 4 large eggs
- 3 tbsp white miso paste
- 4 sea bass fillets, about 6 oz (170g) each, skinned and deboned
- 3 medium red-skinned potatoes
- 12 fresh green beans
- 1 red onion
- 1 medium head of butter lettuce
- 2 large beefsteak tomatoes, sliced
- 16 Kalamata olives, pitted
- 4 tbsp capers
- 2 tbsp chopped fresh flat-leaf parsley
- for the dressing
- 4 garlic cloves, crushed
- 2 tsp Dijon mustard
- 6 tbsp extra virgin olive oil
- 2 tbsp soy sauce
- 2 tbsp white miso
- 3 tbsp rice vinegar
- kosher salt and freshly ground black pepper
- to smoke
- grapevine or apple wood chunks

Directions:

1. Place eggs in a medium saucepan and cover with cold water. Cover the pot with a lid and bring to a boil on the stovetop over high heat. Once boiling, remove the pot from the heat, keep it covered, and let sit for 20 minutes. Drain the water, and set eggs aside to cool. Once cool, peel, halve, and refrigerate until ready to use.
2. To make the dressing, in a small bowl, whisk together garlic, Dijon mustard, oil, soy sauce, miso, and rice vinegar. Season with salt and pepper to taste, and set aside.
3. Preheat the grill to 425°F (218°C) using direct heat with a cast iron grate installed. Add enough water in the dutch oven to cover bass. (Don't add bass to the water yet.) Place the dutch oven on the grate, leave the lid off the dutch oven, and close the grill lid.
4. Once the water starts to simmer, place the wood chunks on the coals. Add miso paste, stirring to dissolve, and then add fish fillets. Leave the lid off the dutch oven, close the grill lid, and cook until cooked through, about 10 minutes per inch of thickness. Remove from the water and set aside.
5. Place potatoes, green beans, and onion on the grate around the dutch oven. Close the lid and grill until charred, about 7 to 10 minutes. Remove the vegetables from the grill, and chop potatoes and onion. Place the vegetables in a medium bowl, add the dressing, and stir to coat.
6. Line a serving platter with the large outer lettuce leaves. Chop the remainder and arrange on the platter. Place tomato slices on one end of the platter, followed by the grilled vegetables. (Don't throw out the dressing from the bowl.) Place fish in the center of the platter. Garnish with sliced hard-boiled eggs, olives, and capers. Sprinkle parsley over top and drizzle the remaining dressing before serving.

Bourbon-glazed Cold Smoked Salmon

Servings: 8 **Cooking Time: 210 Mins.**

Ingredients:

- 2-pound salmon filet, skin on
- 1 tbsp. Makers Mark Bourbon
- 1 orange, zested and sliced into rings
- 1 C. kosher salt
- 2 C. dark brown sugar
- 1 C. Makers Mark Bourbon
- 1/3 C. brown sugar
- ½ C. fig jam
- 1 Tbsp orange juice
- 2 tsp Worcestershire sauce
- ¼ tsp dried mustard
- Pinch of garlic

Directions:

1. Lay the salmon skin-side down on a cutting board. Remove any bones from the flesh and wipe clean of scales. Rinse the salmon with the whiskey and allow to air dry for 10 minutes.
2. In a bowl, combine orange zest, salt and sugar. Line a baking dish with plastic wrap, extending the wrap to allow for wrapping the salmon later. Sprinkle half of the salt mixture on the plastic wrap. Add the salmon and cover with the remaining salt mixture.
3. Lay the orange slices on top of the mixture. Wrap the salmon tightly in the plastic wrap and place in the back of your refrigerator for 48 hours.
4. Once cured, rinse the salmon in cold water. Place the salmon back into the refrigerator, uncovered, for 4 hours.
5. For the glaze, bring bourbon to a boil over medium heat in a saucepan. Add the sugar and whisk, add the remaining ingredients, whisking to blend after each addition. Reduce heat to simmer until sauce is thickened and reduced by half.
6. Preheat the grill to 50°F using direct heat with a cast iron grate installed. Add the salmon to the grid and smoke for 1 hour. Baste the salmon with the bourbon glaze and smoke for an additional 2½ hours.
7. Slice and serve with crackers.

BURGERS RECIPES

Breakfast Burger

Servings: 4 **Cooking Time:** 13 Mins.

Ingredients:

- 1 1/2 lb. ground beef
- 1/2 lb. ground pork breakfast sausage
- 2 tbsp. butter
- 8 strips bacon
- 4 slices sharp cheddar cheese
- 4 Brioche buns
- 4 eggs
- 4 thick slices tomato

Directions:

1. In a medium bowl, mix ground beef and sausage until just combined.
2. Form into 4 patties and refrigerate while the grill heats.
3. Melt butter in a large skillet and fry the eggs for 2 minutes on each side.
4. Grilling:
5. Preheat the grill to 400°F using direct heat with a cast iron grate installed.
6. Place bacon on a small cookie sheet and place on the grid in the grill. Cook until crispy.
7. Place the patties on the grid and close the dome for 3 minutes.
8. Flip the burgers and replace the dome for an additional 3 minutes.
9. Close all of the vents and allow the burgers to sit for an additional 5 minutes. The internal temperature of the burger should be 150°F.
10. Place cheese on top of the burgers and cover for 1 more minute.
11. Assemble the burgers by placing a burger on the bottom bun, topping with bacon, tomato, and a fried egg.

Classic American Burger

Servings: 4 **Cooking Time: 12 Mins.**

Ingredients:

- 2 lbs ground beef
- 1/2 tsp salt
- 1/4 tsp pepper
- 4 slices American cheese
- 4 hamburger buns
- Green Leaf Lettuce
- Sliced Tomato
- Ketchup
- Mustard
- Sliced Pickle

Directions:

1. Form ground beef into four patties and season both sides with salt and pepper.
2. Grilling:
3. Preheat the grill to 500°F using direct heat with a cast iron grate installed.
4. Place burgers on the grid and close the dome for 3 minutes.
5. Flip burgers and close the dome for 2 more minutes.
6. Close all of the vents and allow the burgers to sit for 5 minutes.
7. Top each burger with a slice of cheese and close the dome for 1 more minute.
8. Build burgers with lettuce, tomato, pickle, mustard, and ketchup.

Oahu Burger

Servings: 4 **Cooking Time:** 12 Mins.

Ingredients:

- 2 lbs ground beef
- 1/4 C. thickened Teriyaki Marinade
- 1/4 C. mayonnaise
- 1/2 tsp sambal or sriracha
- 4 slices fresh pineapple, cored
- 4 slices tomato
- 4 slices butter lettuce
- 4 Hawaiian hamburger buns

Directions:

1. Form ground beef into four patties and season both sides with salt and pepper.
2. In a small bowl, mix mayonnaise with hot chile sauce and spread on buns.
3. Top each bun with a burger, slice of pineapple, lettuce and tomato.
4. Grilling:
5. Preheat the grill to 500°F using direct heat with a cast iron grate installed.
6. Place burgers on the grid and close the dome for 3 minutes.
7. Flip burgers, baste with Teriyaki Marinade, and place the pineapple slices on the grid. Close the dome for 2 more minutes.
8. Flip the burgers again and baste with remaining Teriyaki Marinade. Close the dome.
9. Close all of the vents and allow the burgers to sit for 5 minutes.

Quesadilla Burger

Servings: 4 **Cooking Time: 12 Mins.**

Ingredients:

- 2 lbs ground beef
- 2 tbsp. Adobo Rub
- 1 C. shredded cheddar cheese
- 4 large flour tortillas
- Sour Cream
- Guacamole
- Salsa

Directions:

1. Form ground beef into four patties and season both sides with Adobo Rub.
2. Serve each burger with sour cream, guacamole, and salsa.
3. Grilling:
4. Preheat the grill to 500°F using direct heat with a cast iron grate installed.
5. Place burgers on the grid and close the dome for 3 minutes.
6. Flip burgers and close the dome for 2 more minutes.
7. Close all of the vents and allow the burgers to sit for 5 minutes.
8. Remove burgers and place flour tortillas on the grid.
9. Top each tortilla with shredded cheese and close the dome for 1 minute until the cheese melts.
10. Place a hamburger in the center of each tortilla and begin folding the tortilla around the burger like an envelope.

The Crowned Jewels Burger

Servings: 4   **Cooking Time: 12 Mins.**

Ingredients:

- 2 lbs ground beef
- 1/2 tsp salt
- 1/4 tsp pepper
- 1 lb. thinly sliced pastrami
- 1 C. shredded Romaine lettuce
- 1/4 C. mayonnaise
- 2 tbsp. ketchup
- 1/8 tsp onion powder
- 4 slices Sharp Cheddar cheese
- 4 hamburger buns
- 1 tomato, sliced

Directions:

1. Form ground beef into four patties and season both sides with salt and pepper.
2. Meanwhile, mix together mayonnaise, ketchup, and onion powder. Smear on each bun.
3. Place each pastrami and cheese covered burger on the prepared buns and top with shredded lettuce and tomato.
4. Grilling:
5. Preheat the grill to 500°F using direct heat with a cast iron grate installed.
6. Place burgers on the grid and close the dome for 3 minutes.
7. Flip burgers and close the dome for 2 more minutes.
8. Close all of the vents and allow the burgers to sit for 5 minutes.
9. Top each burger with 1/4 of the pastrami and a slice of cheese and close the dome for 1 more minute.

"the Masterpiece"

Servings: 4 **Cooking Time: 12 Mins.**

Ingredients:

- 2 lbs ground beef
- 6 ounces sliced mushrooms
- 4 tbsp. shredded smoked Gouda
- 2 tbsp. butter
- 2 tbsp. olive oil
- 2 tbsp. Dijon mustard
- 1/2 tsp salt
- 1/4 tsp pepper
- 8 slices bacon, cooked and crumbled
- 4 slices Swiss cheese
- 4 brioche buns
- 1 small onion, sliced

Directions:

1. Heat a skillet over medium heat and add 1 tbsp. butter and 1 tbsp. olive oil.
2. Place mushrooms in the pan and DO NOT MOVE THEM. Saute for 5-7 minutes or until the mushrooms are browned. Remove from the pan and set aside.
3. In the same skillet, heat remaining butter and olive oil and add onions. Saute over medium heat until they become translucent and begin to brown, about 10 minutes. Remove from the heat and set aside to cool.
4. Mix onion, mushrooms, and crumbled bacon.
5. Grilling:
6. Preheat the grill to 425°F using direct heat with a cast iron grate installed.
7. Form ground beef into eight patties and season both sides with salt and pepper.
8. Place a generous spoonful of the mushroom and onion mixture in the center of four patties and top with smoked Gouda.
9. Top with additional patty and press sides to seal the mixture inside.
10. Place burgers on the grid and close the dome for 5 minutes.
11. Flip burgers and close the dome for 3 more minutes.
12. Close all of the vents and allow the burgers to sit for 5 minutes.
13. Top each burger with a slice of Swiss cheese and close the dome for 1 more minute.
14. Spread buns with mustard, top with burgers and bun tops.

DESSERTS RECIPES

Seasonal Fruit Cobbler

Servings: 12 **Cooking Time:** 90 Mins.

Ingredients:

- 2 lb. (1kg) seasonal fruit, washed, pitted (if needed), and sliced or halved if needed
- 1/2 tsp ground cinnamon
- 2 tsp cornstarch (for juicy fruits; omit for pears or apples)
- 4 tbsp butter, plus more for greasing
- 1/2 C. sugar, plus more for sprinkling
- 3/4 C. self-rising flour
- 3/4 C. whole milk
- whipped cream, to serve

Directions:

1. Preheat the grill to 350°F (177°C) using indirect heat with a standard grate installed. Place the fruit on the grate (or in a cast iron skillet if the fruit might fall through the grate), close the lid, and grill until beginning to soften and char, about 7 to 10 minutes. Remove fruit from the grill and place in a large bowl. Sprinkle cinnamon and cornstarch (if using) over fruit, and add a little sugar (if desired). Gently toss to coat and set aside.
2. Grease a 9-in (23-cm) grill-safe baking pan with butter. On the stovetop in a small saucepan, heat 4 tbsp butter over medium-low heat until beginning to brown, about 10 to 15 minutes.
3. In a medium bowl, whisk together butter, sugar, flour, and milk. Transfer fruit to the prepared baking pan and spread the batter evenly over top. Place the pan on the grate, close the lid, and bake until golden brown and bubbly, about 1 hour. In the last 10 minutes of cooking, sprinkle a light amount of sugar over top. Remove the cobbler from the grill, and serve warm with whipped cream on top.

Fresh Peach Crisp

Servings: 4 **Cooking Time: 5 Mins.**

Ingredients:

- 2 peaches, halved with pits removed
- Vanilla Ice Cream
- 1 C. good quality granola

Directions:

1. Grilling:
2. Place the peach halves, cut side down, on a 400°F grill and cover with the dome for 5 minutes.
3. Assembly:
4. Remove the peaches and place them, cut side up, in a bowl. Top with vanilla ice cream and granola.

S'mores Pizza

Servings: 8 **Cooking Time: 5 Mins.**

Ingredients:

- 1 pizza dough
- 1/2 C. semi-sweet chocolate chips
- 1/2 C. miniature marshmallows
- 1/4 C. slightly crushed graham crackers

Directions:

1. Stretch dough to a 14" round and place on a pizza peel.
2. Sprinkle dough with chocolate chips, miniature marshmallows, and graham cracker crumbs.
3. Grilling:
4. Slide the pizza onto the prepared stone at 500°F.
5. Cook for 5 minutes, remove from the stone, slice, and serve.

Grilled Sopapillas

Servings: 6 **Cooking Time: 18 Mins.**

Ingredients:

- 1 pizza dough, divided into 6 pieces
- 3 tbsp. melted butter
- 1/4 C. sugar
- 1 tbsp. cinnamon

Directions:

1. Stretch dough into round shape.
2. Place the dough directly on the pizza stone in a 500°F grill.
3. Brush with melted butter and top with cinnamon sugar.
4. Close the dome for 3 minutes, then remove.
5. Repeat with remaining dough.

Apple Pizza

Servings: 8 **Cooking Time: 5 Mins.**

Ingredients:

- 1 pizza dough
- 1 C. apple pie filling
- 1/4 C. vanilla cake mix
- 2 tbsp. melted butter
- Vanilla Ice Cream

Directions:

1. Stretch pizza dough into a 14" round and place on a pizza peel.
2. In a small bowl, combine cake mix and melted butter until it forms a crumbly texture.
3. Spread apple pie filling over pizza dough and top with crumb mixture.
4. Grilling:
5. Bake on a pizza stone in a 500°F grill for 5 minutes.
6. Slice and serve with vanilla frosting.

Corn & Jalapeño Focaccia

Servings: 8 **Cooking Time:** 40 Mins.

Ingredients:

- 2 1/2 C. all-purpose or bread flour
- 1 tbsp kosher salt
- 1/2 tbsp instant dry yeast
- 1 1/2 C. warm water (105°F [41°C])
- 3 tbsp extra virgin olive oil
- 3 jalapeño peppers, left whole
- 1 ear of corn, shucked
- for the butter
- 1 tbsp olive oil
- 2 tbsp unsalted butter
- 4 garlic cloves, minced
- 2 tsp dried oregano
- 1/2 tsp red pepper flakes
- kosher salt

Directions:

1. In a large bowl, combine flour, salt, yeast, and water. Cover tightly with plastic wrap, and set aside to rest for at least 8 hours and up to 24 hours. The dough will rise dramatically and fill the bowl.
2. Pour oil into a large cast iron skillet. Transfer the dough to the skillet, turning the dough to coat in oil. Press the dough around the skillet, flattening slightly and spreading to fill the entire bottom. Cover tightly with plastic wrap and let sit at room temperature for 2 hours.
3. After the first hour, preheat the grill to 425°F (218°C) using indirect heat with a standard grate installed. Place jalapeños and corn on the grate near the edges. Close the lid and grill until beginning to soften and char, about 10 to 12 minutes. Cut the kernels from the cob, and seed and dice jalapeños. Set aside.
4. After resting for 2 hours, the dough should mostly fill the skillet. Use your fingertips to firmly press the dough to the edges, popping any large bubbles that appear. Lift the dough at the edges and allow any air bubbles underneath to escape.
5. Evenly scatter corn and jalapeños over the dough, then push down until they're embedded in the dough. Place the skillet on the grate, close the grill lid, and bake until the top is golden brown and the bottom appears golden brown and crisp when lifted at the edge with a spatula, about 16 to 24 minutes.
6. To make the butter, on the stovetop in a small saucepan over medium-low heat, heat oil and butter until butter melts. Add garlic, oregano, and pepper flakes, and cook for 1 minute, stirring constantly. Transfer to a small bowl and season with salt to taste.
7. Transfer the focaccia to a cutting board and brush the butter over top. Allow to cool slightly, slice, and serve with any remaining butter.

Berry Upside-down Cake

Servings: 10 **Cooking Time:** 30 Mins.

Ingredients:

- 10 tbsp unsalted butter, at room temperature, divided
- 1 C. packed light brown sugar, divided
- 11 oz (315g) fresh seasonal berries
- 1 large egg
- 1 tsp pure vanilla extract
- 2/3 C. sour cream
- 1 1/3 C. all-purpose flour
- 1 tbsp baking powder
- 1/4 tsp baking soda
- 1/2 tsp kosher salt
- 1/4 tsp ground cinnamon
- fresh mint leaves, to garnish
- whipped cream, to serve

Directions:

1. Preheat the grill to 350°F (177°C) using indirect heat with a standard grate installed and a cast iron skillet on the grate. Melt 2 tbsp butter in the skillet and swirl to coat. Remove the skillet from the grill. Sprinkle 1/3 C. brown sugar over butter, pour in berries, and shake the skillet until berries are evenly spread out. Set aside.
2. In the bowl of a stand mixer fitted with the paddle attachment, cream together remaining 8 tbsp butter and 2/3 C. brown sugar until fluffy. Add egg, vanilla, and sour cream, and beat to combine.
3. In a medium bowl, sift together flour, baking powder, baking soda, salt, and cinnamon. Gradually add the dry ingredients to the butter and egg mixture until just incorporated. (The batter will be thick.) Using a rubber spatula, scoop the batter into the skillet, smoothing it over berries.
4. Place the skillet on the grate, close the lid, and bake until golden brown and a cake tester inserted into the middle of the cake comes out clean, about 30 minutes. Remove the skillet from the grill and place on a wire rack to cool for 15 minutes.
5. To serve, flip the cake upside down on a large serving platter and release from the skillet, leaving the berries on top. Garnish with fresh mint leaves, and serve with a dollop of whipped cream.

Death By Chocolate

Servings: 8   **Cooking Time:** 60 Mins.

Ingredients:

- 1 chocolate cake mix, prepared according to package directions
- 2 C. chocolate chips
- 1 C. brown sugar
- 1 1/2 C. water
- 1/2 C. cocoa powder
- 1 (10 oz) bag miniature marshmallows

Directions:

1. Prepare cake mix according to package instructions.
2. Line the dutch oven with a liner.
3. In a medium bowl, combine water, brown sugar, and cocoa powder.
4. Pour the mixture into the bottom of the dutch oven.
5. Top with miniature marshmallows
6. Pour prepared cake mix on top.
7. Top with chocolate chips.
8. Grilling:
9. Preheat the grill to 350°F using direct heat with a cast iron grate installed.
10. Place the lid on the dutch oven and set on the grid of the grill.
11. Close the dome for 1 hour.
12. Remove the dutch oven from the grill, uncover, and serve warm.

Grilled Pineapple Sundaes

Servings: 4 **Cooking Time: 5 Mins.**

Ingredients:

- 4 fresh pineapple spears
- Vanilla Ice Cream
- Jarred Caramel Sauce
- Toasted Coconut

Directions:

1. Place pineapple spears on a 400°F grill and close the dome for 2 minutes.
2. Turn the pineapple and close the dome for another 2 minutes.
3. Turn the pineapple once more and close the dome for another minute.
4. Assembly:
5. Serve pineapple topped with ice cream, caramel sauce, and toasted coconut.

Chocolate Chip Cookie Peanut Butter C. S'mores

Servings: 4 **Cooking Time: 5 Mins.**

Ingredients:

- 8 chocolate chip cookies
- 4 peanut butter C. candies
- 4 marshmallows

Directions:

1. On the grid of a 225°F grill, place one cookie, flat side up, with one peanut butter C. candy and one marshmallow on top.
2. Close the dome for 5 minutes or until the marshmallow begins to puff.
3. Assembly:
4. Close the s'more with the other chocolate chip cookie and get ready for the sugar rush.

SIDES RECIPES

Ratatouille

Servings: 4 **Cooking Time: 30 Mins.**

Ingredients:

- 1/2 C. fresh, shredded basil
- 2 cloves garlic, minced
- 2 large tomatoes, chopped
- 1 red bell pepper, chopped
- 1 large eggplant, peeled and cut into 1/2 inch cubes
- 1 onion, sliced thin
- 1/4 C. olive oil
- 1/4 tsp dried oregano
- 1/4 tsp dried thyme
- 1/4 tsp fennel seeds
- 3/4 tsp salt

Directions:

1. Preheat the grill to 350°F using direct heat with a cast iron grate installed with the dutch oven on the grid.
2. Add olive oil to the pot and toast oregano, thyme, and fennel for 1 minute.
3. Add onion and cook for 5 minutes or until the onion is soft.
4. Add remaining vegetables, cover, and lower the dome for 20-25 minutes.
5. Serve topped with basil.

Roasted Potatoes

Servings: 20 Cooking Time: 30 Mins.

Ingredients:

- 2 lb. (1kg) fingerling potatoes, halved
- 1 tbsp chopped fresh cilantro
- 1 tbsp chopped fresh basil
- 1 tbsp chopped scallions, plus more to garnish
- 3 poblano peppers, diced
- 1/2 C. olive oil
- 1/2 C. white vinegar
- 3 garlic cloves, minced
- kosher salt and freshly ground black pepper
- 1 C. crumbled queso fresco

Directions:

1. Preheat the grill to 425°F (218°C) using indirect heat with a standard grate installed. In a dutch oven or a disposable aluminum baking dish, combine potatoes, cilantro, basil, scallions, peppers, oil, vinegar, and garlic. Toss well to ensure potatoes are coated in oil and seasonings. Place the dutch oven on the grate and cook until potatoes are fork tender, about 30 minutes.
2. Remove the dutch oven from the grill, season with salt and pepper to taste, and top with the queso fresco and more sliced scallions. Serve immediately.

Grilled Lemon Garlic Zucchini

Servings: 6   **Cooking Time:** 5 Mins.

Ingredients:

- 4 zucchini, sliced lengthwise into 1/2 inch slices
- 1/4 C. butter, softened
- 2 tsp parsley, chopped
- 3 cloves garlic, minced
- The zest and juice of 1 lemon

Directions:

1. In a small dish, combine butter, parsley, garlic, lemon zest, and lemon juice.
2. Liberally brush each zucchini slice with the butter mixture.
3. Grilling:
4. Place the zucchini on a 500°F grill and close the dome for 3 minutes.
5. Flip the zucchini and recover with the dome for an additional 2 minutes.
6. Drizzle remaining butter on top of zucchini as it comes off the grill. Serve warm.

Smoked Potato Salad

Servings: 8 **Cooking Time: 120 Mins.**

Ingredients:

- 4 large baking potatoes
- 4 large eggs, hard boiled and finely chopped
- 2 green onions, finely chopped
- 2 large dill pickles, finely chopped
- 1 rib celery, finely diced
- 1/2 C. mayonnaise
- The juice of 1 lemon
- 1/2 tsp black pepper
- 1/2 tsp celery seed
- 1/2 tsp dried dill

Directions:

1. Scrub the potatoes.
2. Grilling:
3. Place the potatoes alongside meat that is smoking at 225°F.
4. Assembly:
5. When the potatoes are fork tender, chill in the refrigerator for 30 minutes.
6. Peel and cut potatoes into small cubes.
7. In a large bowl, combine dressing ingredients.
8. Add potatoes, eggs, green onion, pickle, and celery to the dressing and gently toss

Grilled Onions

Servings: 4 **Cooking Time:** 60 Mins.

Ingredients:

- 4 large sweet onions
- 4 tbsp. butter
- 1 tsp salt
- 1/2 tsp pepper

Directions:

1. Remove the stem end of each onion and peel the skin away.
2. With a melon baller, remove 1 inch of the core of the onion being careful not to disturb the root end.
3. Place 1 tbsp. of butter, 1/4 tsp salt, and 1/8 tsp pepper into each onion.
4. Grilling:
5. Wrap the onions in aluminum foil and place on a 225°F grill for 1 hour with the dome closed.
6. Unwrap the onions and serve warm.

Baba Ganoush

Servings: 8 **Cooking Time: 10 Mins.**

Ingredients:

- 2 tbsp. fresh parsley
- 1 eggplant, sliced into 1/2 inch rounds
- 1 clove garlic
- The juice and zest of 1 lemon
- 2 tbsp. olive oil
- 2 tbsp. tahini
- Salt & Pepper

Directions:

1. Brush both sides of each eggplant slice with olive oil and season with salt and pepper.
2. Preheat the grill to 425°F using direct heat with a cast iron grate installed and close the dome for 3-5 minutes.
3. Flip the eggplant and close the dome for another 3-5 minutes.
4. Assembly:
5. Peel the eggplant skins away from the flesh and discard.
6. In a food processor, combine eggplant, tahini, parsley, garlic, lemon zest and lemon juice and puree until smooth.
7. Taste for seasoning and add salt and pepper accordingly.
8. Serve at room temperature with pita chips, pretzels, or raw vegetables.

Cowboy Potatoes

Servings: 6 **Cooking Time: 60 Mins.**

Ingredients:

- 2 lbs Russet potatoes, very thinly sliced
- 1/2 lb. bacon, diced
- 2 C. cheddar cheese
- 1 onion, thinly sliced
- 1 tsp salt
- 1/2 tsp pepper

Directions:

1. Preheat the grill to 375°F using direct heat with a cast iron grate installed with the dutch oven on the grid.
2. Add bacon and cook until crisp.
3. Add onion and cook for 3 minutes until it begins to soften.
4. Add sliced potatoes and gently stir to coat the potatoes in the bacon fat. Season with salt and pepper
5. Cover the dutch oven and lower the dome for 40 minutes or until the potatoes are soft.
6. Remove the cover and top with cheese. Replace the cover and allow the dutch oven to sit off the heat for another 2-3 minutes until the cheese is melted.

Mac And Cheese

Servings: 6 **Cooking Time:** 60 Mins.

Ingredients:

- 1 lb. smoked cheddar cheese, shredded, divided
- 1/4 C. butter
- 2 eggs
- 1/2 lb. elbow macaroni
- 3/4 C. evaporated milk
- 1/4 C. Panko breadcrumbs
- 1 tsp salt
- 3/4 tsp dry mustard

Directions:

1. In a large pot of boiling, salted water cook the macaroni according to package directions and drain.
2. In a separate bowl, whisk together the eggs, milk, hot sauce, salt, pepper, and mustard.
3. Grilling:
4. Preheat the grill to 350°F using direct heat with a cast iron grate installed with the dutch oven on the grid.
5. Melt the butter in the dutch oven and place macaroni in the pot. Toss to coat.
6. Stir the egg and milk mixture into the pasta and add half of the cheese.
7. Continuously stir the mac and cheese for 3 minutes or until creamy.
8. Top with remaining cheese and Panko breadcrumbs.
9. Cover the dutch oven, lower the dome, and cook for 20-25 minutes.
10. Serve immediately.

Grilled Cabbage With Champagne Vinaigrette

Servings: 6 **Cooking Time: 10 Mins.**

Ingredients:

- » 1 head cabbage
- » 2 tbsp. olive oil
- » Salt and Pepper
- » 1/2 C. olive oil
- » 1/4 C. Champagne vinegar
- » 2 tbsp. capers in brine, drained
- » 1 tbsp. Dijon mustard
- » 1 shallot, finely chopped

Directions:

1. Cut the cabbage into 1/2 inch "steaks" from top to root.
2. Brush each side with olive oil and season with salt and pepper.
3. Grilling:
4. Preheat the grill to 425°F using direct heat with a cast iron grate installed and close the lid for 5 minutes.
5. Meanwhile, in a small bowl, combine shallot, mustard, capers, and vinegar.
6. While whisking, stream in olive oil until dressing emulsifies.
7. Flip cabbage steaks and cook on the other side for an additional 5 minutes with the dome closed.
8. Remove cabbage from the grill to a platter and pour dressing over top. Serve warm.

Dutch Oven Black Beans

Servings: 6   **Cooking Time: 40 Mins.**

Ingredients:

- 1 medium yellow onion, peeled and halved
- 1 green bell pepper, left whole
- 2 x 15 oz (425g) cans black beans with liquid or 3 C. cooked black beans
- 2 garlic cloves, minced
- 1 tsp ground cumin
- 1/2 tsp dried oregano
- 1/2 tsp kosher salt
- 1 tsp red wine vinegar
- 1 bunch of fresh cilantro, chopped

Directions:

1. Preheat the grill to 350°F using direct heat with a cast iron grate installed and a dutch oven on the grate. Arrange onions and pepper on the grate around the dutch oven, close the grill lid, and grill until beginning to soften and char, about 5 to 7 minutes. Transfer the vegetables to a cutting board and chop.
2. Add 1/8 C. bean liquid to the dutch oven. Add onion, pepper, and garlic, close the grill lid, and sauté until soft, about 2 minutes. Add beans with the remaining liquid. Stir in cumin, oregano, and salt. Cover the dutch oven with its lid and close the grill lid. Simmer for 15 to 30 minutes.
3. Remove the dutch oven from the grill and stir in the vinegar and cilantro, reserving a bit to sprinkle over top. Serve immediately.

Printed in Great Britain
by Amazon